The
Chinese
Shar-Pei

Reddith Jo Ann Thrower

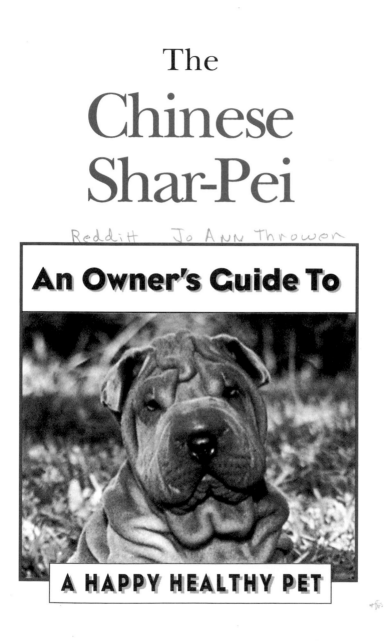

An Owner's Guide To

A HAPPY HEALTHY PET

Howell Book House

Howell Book House
A Simon & Schuster Macmillan Company
1633 Broadway
New York, NY 10019

MACMILLAN is a registered trademark of Macmillan, Inc.

Library of Congress Cataloging-in-Publication Data
Redditt, Jo Ann Thrower.
The Chinese Shar-Pei: an owner's guide to a happy, healthy pet/
Jo Ann Redditt.
p. cm.

ISBN 0-87605-396-7

1. Chinese Shar-Pei. I. Title.
SF429.C48R42 1996
636.7'2—dc20   95-46192
                   CIP

Manufactured in the United States of America
10 9 8 7 6 5 4 3 2 1

Series Director: Dominique De Vito
Series Assistant Editor: Ariel Cannon
Book Design: Michele Laseau
Cover Design: Iris Jeromnimon
Illustration: Jeff Yesh
Photography:
  Cover: *Paulette Braun/Pets by Paulette*
  Courtesy of Ken-L Ration: 93
  Madeline Albright: 21·
  Joan Balzarini: 96
  Mary Bloom: 96, 136, 145
  Paulette Braun/Pets by Paulette: 12, 25, 32–33, 34, 42, 44, 53, 58
  Buckinghamhill American Cocker Spaniels: 148
  Sian Cox: 134
  Dr. Ian Dunbar: 98, 101, 103, 111, 116–117, 122, 123, 127
  Alan Klessig: 5, 8, 13, 19, 22, 62, 74, 77
  Rosie Lucitt: 17
  Dan Lyons: 96
  Cathy Merrithew: 129
  Liz Palika: 133
  Janice Raines: 132
  Jo Ann Redditt: 10, 15, 20, 23, 43, 48, 60
  Barbara Roche: 28, 39, 41, 55, 57, 59
  Ted Schiffman: 54
  Morna Stockman: 37
  Judith Strom: 14, 30, 36, 96, 107, 110, 128, 130, 135, 137, 139, 140, 144, 149, 150
  Anita Utley: 18
  Jean Wentworth: 2–3, 24
  Kerrin Winter & Dale Churchill: 96–97

Contents

Welcome

to the

World

of the

part one

Chinese Shar-Pei

External Features of the Shar-Pei

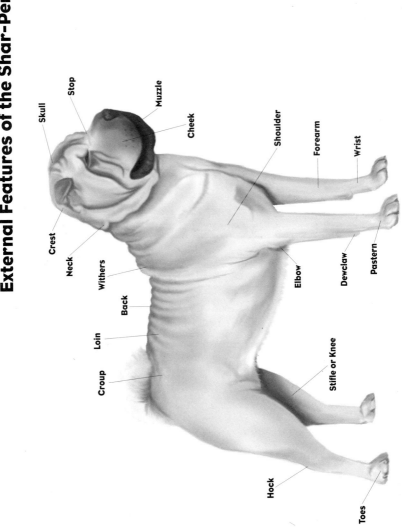

Skull · Stop · Muzzle · Cheek · Crest · Neck · Withers · Back · Loin · Croup · Shoulder · Forearm · Wrist · Elbow · Dewclaw · Pastern · Stifle or Knee · Hock · Toes

What

Is a

Chinese Shar-Pei?

What Is a Standard?

In order to understand a breed standard, one must first have an elementary knowledge of dogs. One should know a croup from the withers and a stifle from a hock, and also be able to understand the utilitarian purpose for which a breed was "designed." Efficiency usually sets the standard

for any breed. Those animals who performed best for a given task were bred to others with similar qualities. Characteristics required to complete the master's tasks were deliberately bred into the dog.

The standard of excellence of any breed is the only guide by which we preserve a breed. It is a word picture that describes an ideal whole. Unfortunately, the minor details are sometimes emphasized at the expense of what should be more fundamental—such as soundness, balance and total conformation. The ideal for any dog must encompass features of type and soundness.

WHAT IS A BREED STANDARD?

A breed standard—a detailed description of an individual breed—is meant to portray the *ideal* specimen of that breed. This includes ideal structure, temperament, gait, type—all aspects of the dog. Because the standard describes an ideal specimen, it isn't based on any particular dog. It is a concept against which judges compare actual dogs and breeders strive to produce dogs. At a dog show, the dog that wins is the one that comes closest, in the judge's opinion, to the standard for its breed. Breed standards are written by the breed parent clubs, the national organizations formed to oversee the well-being of the breed. They are voted on and approved by the members of the parent clubs.

This is certainly true with Shar-Pei. How many times have you heard, "I just love those Shar-Pei puppies, but when they grow up they lose their wrinkles! Wouldn't it be nice if you could keep them puppies forever?" To achieve this, and because there is a market for these dogs, some breeders breed the most wrinkled dog to another very wrinkled dog, thereby trying to increase wrinkling in adult dogs. Some may breed the smallest dogs together in attempts to breed a so-called "mini-Pei." Some of these breeders have discovered that the smallest is not as large as his littermates because of some health problem (such as malabsorption). The end result may be a smaller or more wrinkled Shar-Pei, but not necessarily a sound or healthy Shar-Pei. If the dog cannot properly digest food, he will naturally be smaller. Is this what we really want? While it is true that many breeds have been "miniaturized," it takes knowledgeable breeders with years of experience to accomplish such a task successfully.

A standard describes, trait by trait, those features that make up type and soundness, but an experienced student of any breed will assess the animal as a complete entity. The dog must have good conformation to the standard, solid structure and the ability for each of these parts to function harmoniously and efficiently with all the other parts.

The Chinese Shar-Pei Club of America Official Standard

Those who sought to write an American standard of perfection for the Chinese Shar-Pei deliberately omitted any reference to dogfighting, which had been included in the original Hong Kong Standard. Rather, they sought to describe a compact, close-coupled dog—a muscular, strong dog of medium size who would perhaps be a guard dog or hunting companion. It is believed that the Shar-Pei was originally a peasant dog raised in the countryside to help his owner in these pursuits. The most recent standard, which follows, was approved by the CSPCA (Chinese Shar-Pei Club of America) and became effective on January 1, 1988. This standard is the first one to contain four disqualifications for the breed when it is judged in the showring. Contact the AKC (see Resources, chapter 13) for a complete copy of the Shar-Pei Standard.

In the following presentation of the Official CSPCA Standard, you will find interpretive comments that are the opinions of this author only. They are meant to help the novice fancier who wishes to understand how to translate the language of a standard to more common usage.

General Appearance—An alert, dignified, active, compact dog of medium size and substance, square in profile, close-coupled, the well proportioned head slightly but not overly large for the body. The short, harsh coat, the loose skin covering the head and body, the small ears, the "hippopotamus" muzzle shape and the high set tail impart to the Shar-Pei a unique look peculiar to him alone. The loose skin and wrinkles covering the head, neck and body are superabundant in puppies but these features may be limited to the head, neck and withers in the adult.

Comment: The Shar-Pei should be a square-bodied dog (further described in "Body," below) with all his parts in proportion to each other. An adult dog should not be profusely wrinkled over the entire body as are puppies. In adults, the wrinkling is limited to the head and shoulders and is only moderate or minimal on the rest of the body.

Head—Large, slightly but not overly, proudly carried and covered with profuse wrinkles on the forehead continuing into side wrinkles framing the face. *Skull*—Flat and broad, the stop is moderately defined, the length from nose to stop is approximately the same as from stop to occiput. *Muzzle*—One of the distinctive features of the breed. It is broad and full with no suggestion of snipiness. The lips and top of muzzle are well padded and may cause a slight bulge at the base of the nose. *Nose*—Large and wide and darkly pigmented, preferably black but any color nose conforming to the general coat color of the dog is acceptable. In dilute colors, the preferred nose is self-colored. Darkly pigmented cream Shar-Pei may have some light pigment either in the center of their noses or on their entire nose. *Teeth*—Strong, meeting in a scissors bite. Deviation from a scissor bite is a major fault. *Eyes*—Dark, small, almond-shaped and sunken, displaying a scowling expression. In dilute dogs, the eye color may be lighter. *Ears*—Extremely small rather thick, equilateral triangles in shape, slight rounded at the tips, edges of the ear may curl. Ears lie flat against the head, are set wide apart and forward on the skull, pointing toward the eyes. The ears have the ability to move. Pricked ears are a disqualification. *Tongue, Roof of Mouth, Gums and Flews*—A solid bluish-black is preferred in all coat colors except the dilute colors which have solid lavender pigmentation.

Even at a young age, this Shar-Pei has all the independence and confidence that make the breed attractive.

Comment: The adult Shar-Pei head, while large in proportion to the body, should not be so large as to be totally out of proportion. It should retain some wrinkles, which continue to form moderate dewlaps under the chin; it should not be so grossly wrinkled that one cannot see the eyes of the dog, or so that the dog is prevented from seeing the world around him. The muzzle should be full and broad, sometimes with a bulge at the top of the muzzle just above the nose. This is distinctive in the Shar-Pei, and the standard is a little ambiguous in describing the bulge at the "base" of the nose. The teeth should have a "scissors bite," with the top teeth closing tightly over the bottom teeth and the canine teeth overlapping like a pair of scissors. Other types of bites (undershot, overshot or level) are considered major faults.

The ears should be small (some have even been described as small as a thumbnail) and close to the head: small triangles pointing at the eyes except for those that curl up at the edges (and this is acceptable). Pricked ears (ears that stand up and away from the head as in a German Shepherd Dog or Siberian Husky) are a disqualification. The tongue should be bluish-black (except in the dilutes, in which case the standard calls for lavender), and as much of the mouth as possible should be of the same color.

Body—*Proportion*—The height of a Shar-Pei from the ground to the withers is approximately equal to the length from point of breastbone to point of rump. *Neck*—Medium length, full and set well into the shoulders. There are moderate to heavy folds of loose skin and abundant dewlap about the neck and throat. *Back*—Short and close-coupled, the topline dips slightly behind the withers, slight rising over the short, broad loin. *Chest*—Broad and deep with the brisket extending to the elbow and rising slightly under the loin. *Croup*—Flat, with the base of the tail set extremely high, clearly exposing an uptilted anus. *Tail*—The high set tail is a characteristic feature of the Chinese Shar-Pei. The tail is thick and round at the base, tapering to a fine point and curling over or to either side of the back. The absence of a complete tail is a disqualification.

Comment: The "squareness" of the Shar-Pei is described in this portion of the Standard. The proportion of the height to the length should be equal. The neck is of medium length, not too long or appearing as if the head is set directly on the shoulders, but instead set well into the shoulders and gently sloping without interruption. The wrinkles may be uniform over the head, neck and withers, the coat gradually becoming smooth over the back. The topline, when viewed in profile, dips slightly behind the withers where the wrinkling ends and rises slowly to the tail, but there should be no suggestion of a roached (humped) back. The unique Shar-Pei tail should be thick and round at the base, tapering to a finepoint, and must always be thrust forward in a curl (the degree of curl not defined) to either side. Less-desirable tails would be described as "stovepipe" or "periscope" (sticking straight up), or pointing away from the body. The absence of a complete tail—no tail or a stub tail—is a disqualification.

The Chinese Shar-Pei is an "alert and dignified" dog.

Forequarters—Shoulders—Muscular, well laid back and sloping. *Forelegs—*When viewed from the front, straight, moderately spaced, with elbows close to the body. When viewed from the side, the forelegs are straight, the pasterns are strong and flexible. The bone is substantial but never heavy and is of moderate length. *Feet—*Moderate in size, compact and firmly set; not splayed. Removal of front dewclaws is optional.

Comment: When seen from the front in a natural position, a Shar-Pei's legs should come down in a straight line from the body and be moderately spaced, with the elbows close to the body (some Shar-Pei may be "out at the elbows," and this is undesirable). The pasterns (ankles) should be strong, yet flexible, and not weak or "let down." The feet should be compact and well knuckled up, not splayed or too large. Removal of the front dewclaws is optional, but most breeders opt to do so.

Hindquarters—Muscular, strong, and moderately angulated. The metatarsals (hocks) are short, perpendicular to the ground and parallel to each other when viewed from the rear. Hind dewclaws must be removed.

Comment: This description of the rear is well stated and very clear. There should be no hint of weakness in the rear and the feet should be well knuckled up and not splayed. Not all Shar-Pei are born with rear dewclaws, but some are (some even have double dewclaws at birth), and these should be removed.

Coat—The extremely harsh coat is one of the distinguishing features of the breed. The coat is absolutely straight and offstanding on the main trunk of the body but generally lies somewhat flatter on the limbs. The coat appears healthy without being shiny or lustrous. Acceptable coat lengths may range from extremely short "horse" coat up to a "brush" coat length not to exceed one inch in length at the withers. A soft coat, a wavy coat, a coat in excess of one inch in length at the withers, a coat that has been trimmed *is a major fault.* The Shar-Pei is shown in a natural state.

THE AMERICAN KENNEL CLUB

Familiarly referred to as "the AKC," the American Kennel Club is a nonprofit organization devoted to the advancement of pure-bred dogs. The AKC maintains a registry of recognized breeds and adopts and enforces rules for dog events including shows, obedience trials, field trials, hunting tests, lure coursing, herding, earthdog trials, agility and the Canine Good Citizen program. It is a club of clubs, established in 1884 and composed, today, of over 500 autonomous dog clubs throughout the United States. Each club is represented by a delegate; the delegates make up the legislative body of the AKC, voting on rules and electing directors. The American Kennel Club maintains the Stud Book, the record of every dog ever registered with the AKC, and publishes a variety of materials on purebred dogs, including a monthly magazine, books and numerous educational pamphlets. For more information, contact the AKC at the address listed in Chapter 13, "Resources," and look for the names of their publications in Chapter 12, "Recommended Reading."

Comment: The texture of the coat should be harsh; in shorter coats, which may be as short as one-fourth inch, even prickly. Even the brushcoat should be harsh, with no undercoat. The length is not to exceed one inch at the withers, meaning the coat on the rest of the body should be less than one inch. So-called "Bear Coats" do exist, most likely throwbacks to the Chow Chow, and are unacceptable as they have an undercoat and a length that exceeds one inch. The Shar-Pei is shown in its natural state, and coats should never be trimmed.

Shar-Pei come in many different and striking colors, though not all combinations are acceptable in the showring.

Color—Only solid colors are acceptable. A solid colored dog may have shading, primarily darker down the back and on the ears. The shading must be variations of the same body color (except in sables) and may include darker hairs throughout the coat. The following are disqualifications: albino, brindle, parti-color (patches), spotted (spots, ticked, roaning), and a tan-pointed pattern (typical black and tan or saddled).

Comment: With approximately twelve distinctly different colors of Shar-Pei being acceptable, it is understandable why many find what is not acceptable confusing. If one keeps in mind that there are two groups of colors, the "basic colors" and the "dilutes," each consisting of six colors that are solid colors, it may be a little easier to remember. The acceptable basic colors are solid colors, all with some black (or charcoal) pigmentation in the muzzle, skin, nose, tongue, flews and footpads (the nails may be darker). These colors may be darker shades on the ears and along the center of the back and are as follows: cream, fawn, red, brown, sable, black. There should be no delineation of color (as in tan-pointed dogs, such as Dobermans).

The second group of colors are the dilutes, or what may be called "self-colored" dogs. Included in this group are the creams, apricots, five-point reds, chocolates, sables and silvers—all with the dilute description following the color name (for example, cream dilute). This group of dogs has *no* black (or charcoal) pigmentation anywhere. The skin, nose, muzzle and nails are all the same color as the coat. The eyes may be light or dark, and the tongues may vary from light to dark lavender.

Gait—The movement of a Shar-Pei is to be judged at a trot. The gait is free and balanced with the feet tending to converge on a center line of gravity when the dog moves at a vigorous trot. The gait combines good forward reach and strong drive in hindquarters. Proper movement is essential.

A well-proportioned Shar-Pei moves with agility and grace.

Comment: A Shar-Pei with the correct angulation in his shoulders, a strong neck of moderate length (not too short), a strong and muscular rear with good angulation, legs normally positioned straight under the body, and who is fairly compact in body, will move with an effortless, fluid motion, with good reach in the front and a strong drive from the rear. This animal is a pleasure to watch when he moves at a trot.

Size—The preferred height is 18 to 20 inches at the withers. The preferred weight is 40 to 55 pounds. The dog is usually larger and more square bodied than the bitch but both appear well proportioned.

Comment: Keep in mind that the length of coat greatly affects appearance. The brushcoated dogs may appear taller and larger than they really are. It is far more difficult for the short, horse-coated dog to hide any of his shortcomings.

Shar-Pei's coarse, short coats do not need trimming or elaborate grooming to look superb in the showring.

Temperament—Regal, alert, intelligent, dignified, lordly, scowling, sober and snobbish, essentially independent and somewhat standoffish with strangers, but extreme in his devotion to his family. The Shar-Pei stands firmly on the ground with a calm confident stature.

Comment: It is difficult for one dog to live up to all the descriptions under "Temperament," but many Shar-Pei do. Some are extremely friendly and never know a stranger, but the majority will be somewhat standoffish until they have "sized up" an individual. They also make excellent family dogs and will guard the house with diligence. In general, they are very intelligent and independent, tending to set their own standards and accepting those of their owners with time. Once dominance is established, they will accept the will of their master.

chapter 2

The
Chinese Shar-Pei's
Ancestry

Much of the history of the Chinese Shar-Pei is unknown, and a great deal of what has been written is conjecture. While there are ancient Chinese statues that resemble the Shar-Pei, they could also be of the Chow Chow or the Pug. Since Chinese culture has not historically valued the dog, there are no reliable pedigree records available to trace the genealogy of this breed prior to its arrival in the United States. Most Shar-Pei in the United States were exported from Hong Kong, Taiwan or Macao, but because of the lack of interest in organized kennel activities and

because of the internal struggles in China, most of the Shar-Pei were non-pedigreed, and little was known of their history.

There is no strong evidence to prove either that the Shar-Pei is an ancient breed or a more recent combination of breeds, only hints at both possibilities. While the blue-black tongue suggests a connection with the Chow Chow, the rest of the Chinese Shar-Pei's genetic makeup is conjecture.

WHERE DID DOGS COME FROM?

It can be argued that dogs were right there at man's side from the beginning of time. As soon as human beings began to document their existence, the dog was among their drawings and inscriptions. Dogs were not just friends, they served a purpose: There were dogs to hunt birds, pull sleds, herd sheep, burrow after rats—even sit in laps! What your dog was originally bred to do influences the way it behaves. The American Kennel Club recognizes over 140 breeds, and there are hundreds more distinct breeds around the world. To make sense of the breeds, they are grouped according to their size or function. The AKC has seven groups:

1) Sporting, 2) Working,
3) Herding, 4) Hounds,
5) Terriers, 6) Toys,
7) Nonsporting

Can you name a breed from each group? Here's some help: (1) Golden Retriever; (2) Doberman Pinscher; (3) Collie; (4) Beagle; (5) Scottish Terrier; (6) Maltese; and (7) Dalmatian. All modern domestic dogs (*Canis familiaris*) are related, however different they look, and are all descended from *Canis lupus*, the gray wolf.

Original Purposes of the Breed

It is believed that the Shar-Pei was originally a peasant dog, and its strong, muscular build indicates that it may have been used for guarding and hunting and later, for pit fighting in the southern regions of China. I have been told by a Chinese gentleman who immigrated to this country that when he was a child, his father took him to a dogfight in Beijing where he saw his first Shar-Pei. The incident made him sick. (Today, that gentleman is a respected AKC judge, Mr. Richard T'ang.)

Bringing the Breed to the U.S.

We do know that in the late 1960s, a young Chinese man named Matgo Law took on the difficult task of trying to save an almost extinct breed that had been decimated by famine, high taxes, prejudice and the sport of dogfighting. Chinese gamblers, who recognized and wished to improve the dog's value as a pit fighter, had crossbred other champion combatants with the Shar-Pei, thus mongrelizing the breed. Matgo Law had to travel far and wide to try to find specimens who resembled the Shar-Pei, and he faced the considerable task of trying to purify the breed.

The now-famous appeal by Matgo Law of Down-Homes Kennels, Hong Kong, appeared in *Dogs* magazine in April 1973. In this article, Law begged the canine fancy in the United States to help save the Shar-Pei who, listed as the "rarest dog in the world" by the *Guinness Book of Records*, would otherwise become extinct.

Two early Chinese Shar-Pei. On the right is Down Homes China Souel, the first Shar-Pei to be registered with the CSPCA; his daughter, Albright's Min Yung is on the left.

In answer to Matgo Law's plea, a few Shar-Pei began to trickle into the U.S. The first Shar-Pei to be registered with the CSPCA was Down-Homes China Souel, owned by Ernest and Madeline Albright of California, as was the first registered litter.

The breed's registration was established in 1974 with the Chinese Shar-Pei Club of America, Inc., when a group of owners and fanciers held its first organizational meeting, with Ernest Albright elected as president.

Without question, Down-Homes Kennels played the biggest role in promoting and establishing the Chinese Shar-Pei in the United States and indeed, in the world, but other names played an important role in early imports as well. Chinese Diamond Kennels, owned by Yu Ying Wai, and Gun Club Kennels, owned by Robert Horsnell, were also integral in establishing the Shar-Pei in this country.

**FAMOUS
OWNERS OF
CHINESE
SHAR-PEI**

Yul Brynner

Geraldo
Rivera

Wayne
Newton

Jerry
Weintraub

The King of
Saudi Arabia

Growth and Popularity in the U.S.

Since the arrival of the first few Chinese Shar-Pei on our shores, the breed has experienced a most phenomenal growth in popularity and consequently, in population. Because of its unique appearance, it has been sought after by the American public, often as a fad item. Neither price nor quality seem to deter the fanciers of this breed. We see Shar-Pei in commercials for perfume, cosmetics that tout a non-wrinkling agent, clothes, cards, steam irons, dog food and bleach. In magazines, the list of commercial advertisers who use photographs of the Shar-Pei to sell their products is even more lengthy.

Shar-Pei have been competing in all AKC licensed events since the breed was recognized in 1992. This pair is participating in Junior Showmanship.

Its faddish popularity has encouraged those who would be breeders to produce puppies at an alarming rate. The American Kennel Club reports that as of February 28, 1995, there are 127,666 Chinese Shar-Pei registered, and an average of 1,300 new Shar-Pei are registered every month. If you consider that not every puppy born is registered, a conservative estimate of the Shar-Pei population in the United States would be twice the number of registered Shar-Pei.

With these numbers, the Chinese Shar-Pei can no longer be considered a "rare" breed. On August 1, 1992, the breed was allowed to compete in AKC licensed events, taking its place as the 134th breed to be recognized by the American Kennel Club. Its rapidly growing population is evident in the fact that it is not uncommon to find a Shar-Pei in an animal shelter either picked up as a stray or turned in by its owner. Shar-Pei rescue groups have organized all over the country to help place the unwanted, abused and neglected members of the breed. In our area of Washington, D.C., we have placed over 300 rescue Shar-Pei in the last five years.

THE PRICE OF BEING A FAD

The popularity of an item does not ensure its quality. Actually, quite the reverse is usually the case. A larger quantity of that item is produced to meet an ever-growing demand, and unfortunately, mass production tends to reduce the quality of a product. This maxim is particularly true when one is dealing with living beings rather than inanimate objects. Some breeders do not take the time or the effort to educate themselves about the background of their breeding stock, investigate the lineage of potential studs, or learn about genetics. Health and temperament problems can result from such poor planning.

Fortunately, as time has passed and the fad factor has diminished, many of the entrepreneurs have moved on to "richer pastures," leaving a solid core of dedicated breeders who are determined to eliminate some of the health problems that have plagued the Chinese Shar-Pei. Today, the new Shar-Pei owner has a better of chance of purchasing a healthy, well-tempered dog.

The Shar-Pei has traits in common with both the Mastiff and the Chow Chow.

When I first began showing my Shar-Pei in the conformation ring, it was not unusual to see one or more dogs excused from the showring for temperament problems—growling, snapping at the judge or threatening another Shar-Pei. Today this behavior is an extremely unusual occurrence. Most judges will tell you that the Shar-Pei is one of the better-behaved breeds in the showring today. This can be directly traced to careful breeding practices.

Chinese Shar-Pei Versatility

I would be remiss if I did not mention the many events and activities in which the Shar-Pei excels. Shar-Pei take to obedience training like Border Collies to herding. They excel in Agility; many are registered with Therapy Dogs International, where they visit nursing homes, schools and other groups, spreading their special brand of cheer. Some are excellent Tracking dogs,

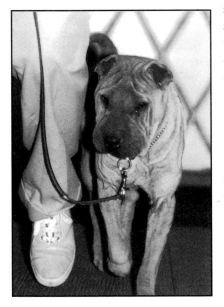

and others have proved capable as "hearing-ear dogs." I have yet to hear of a Shar-Pei who was successfully trained as a seeing-eye dog, but I'm sure there must be at least one out there; they have the intelligence and devotion needed for this task. There is at least one Schutzhund-titled Shar-Pei: Ling Chiu's Mr. Magoo. And Ann Nowicki of Phoenix, Arizona, has trained and used her Shar-Pei to herd sheep in addition to performing obedience and agility activities.

The first Shar-Pei to earn an obedience title was Hon. Ch. Linn's Ping, who was awarded her CD (a

Danros U-Woof-O was the first Chinese Shar-Pei to be registered with Therapy Dogs International.

CSPCA title) in 1981. At the age of ten, she earned yet another obedience Companion Dog title, this time under AKC auspices.

The first lady of training obedience-titled Chinese Shar-Pei is Rosie Lucitt, who titled the first honorary CDX Shar-Pei, Fritts' Han-Ho-Yan. His daughter, Danros U-Woof-O, was the first Shar-Pei to receive an official CDX from the American Kennel Club and the first of her breed to be registered with Therapy Dogs International.

Now, our breed can boast of another "first." On September 4, 1994, Ch. Nantru's First Emperor ("Bubba"), owned by Marla Gularte, became the first UDX (Utility Dog Excellent) Chinese Shar-Pei.

Even though the recorded history of the Shar-Pei is relatively brief, obscure and littered with certain undesirable chapters, the breed came to our shores with a plea to save it from extinction, and save it we did, in good ol' American fashion. In turn, it has shown us it can be the most versatile and intelligent of dogs.

About 1,300 Chinese Shar-Pei puppies are registered every month with the AKC.

chapter 3

The **World**

According to the
Chinese Shar-Pei

Many of the traits of early Shar-Pei, such as an innate intelligence and a keen perceptiveness, were desirable and have been retained in today's Shar-Pei. The Shar-Pei is very alert and highly responsive, but in excess, these characteristics can produce a highly strung, sensitive and somewhat reserved animal. The breeder's challenge in the United States was to breed out those less desirable characteristics while keeping those that endeared the breed to its fanciers.

Today, the Shar-Pei has proven that that her innate intelligence is challenged when presented with worthwhile goals, and that her dedication to her master endows her with a willingness to please and participate in any activity where praise is her reward.

The Shar-Pei as a Guard Dog

The breed seems to be well suited to this purpose as Shar-Pei seem to accept their home area quickly and establish boundary areas that they will actively defend. However, Rosie Lucitt, an experienced trainer and Shar-Pei breeder, says, "I believe that the independence factor in the Shar-Pei makes the breed an unsuitable choice for guard-dog training. The instinct to naturally protect is there, but to guard 'on command' usually meets with resistance. I found that not only are they instinctively protective, but they enjoy their work. This probably is the hindrance to guard training as while they are working, they are very easily 'carried away'

and what should have been an inhibited protective action (e.g., fierce barking, but no attack) turns to frenzy. This is not to say they won't 'guard' as most people interpret the function. Most certainly, a Shar-Pei will bark at strangers and be an excellent 'burglar alarm' in his home. The question is, 'How far will he go?' Is his protective instinct readily controllable? What can be done about the high intensity of their aggressive reactions? And realistically, is that what you want the cute, wrinkley puppy to do?"

Shar-Pei soon become loyal family members.

This does not mean that every Shar-Pei has an aggressive nature. Many are sweet, docile couch potatoes throughout their lives!

The Shar-Pei as a Hunter

Most historical references to the Chinese Shar-Pei mention the dog being used to hunt wild boar, or, in one case, the mongoose. While there is little demand for boar hunters in the United States, I find no reason

Shar-Pei's excellent noses are well suited to hunting—or just playing!

why a Shar-Pei would not make an excellent hunting dog for other game. They have already proven adept at the basic concepts necessary for a good hunting dog: attention, sit, come, retrieve, heel. All of my Shar-Pei love playing ball and with a little patience will soon learn to retrieve the ball, drop it at my feet and, tail wagging, wait with tensed muscle to retrieve it again. Most have a good, sensitive nose and tracking ability, intelligence, and the strong desire to please the master. Our first Shar-Pei, Down-Homes Prophet, would often suddenly awake from a sound asleep, lift his head, sniff the air (all windows were closed, mind you) and let us know that a cat had passed through our yard. Upon checking, we found that he was always right!

It may also be argued, however, that the same instinct that prevents the Shar-Pei from becoming a reliable guard dog could also take hold when the dog has game in his mouth. Independent Shar-Pei may respond to their own strong instincts rather than obey their master's orders.

The Shar-Pei as a Herding Dog

It has been said that the Shar-Pei was also used for herding in its native land. One Shar-Pei breeder, Ann Nowicki, owner of Haleakala Kennels in Phoenix, Arizona, told about her "Shar-Pei Shepherds" in the First Quarterly 1992 issue of *The Orient Express II*, a magazine for the Chinese Shar-Pei:

My Shar-Pei, Niblets, has always displayed some herding ability at home. She would keep any litter of puppies together in a group. She would also 'herd' my smooth Chow, Kristy, all over the back yard. Niblets needed a little encouragement the first time she was on sheep. She wasn't quite sure what she was supposed to do or even what the sheep were. This is not unusual as even traditional herding breeds may require three to four exposures to stock before they get the idea. But Niblets learned very quickly. She instinctively moved to the front of the flock to turn them and would stay back off the stock.

Herding is the most difficult event I have done with the dogs. Not only do you have to watch the dog, you also have to watch the stock and be able to read the animals. We have been herding for a little over a year now and both dogs enjoy it immensely and have improved considerably. I'm sure a flock of their own is at the top of their wish lists! There were occasions when I thought none of us would ever get the hang of it. Now that my dogs and I have it all together, it is such a feeling of accomplishment because we have done a job together and also because a Chow and a Shar-Pei can still perform the work they did many years ago in China.

Some Shar-Pei are happy to spend the day snoozing.

A Breed in Transition

Because the breed is still in transition, this is perhaps the most important piece of advice I can give: It can be foolhardy to generalize as to the health and especially the temperament of the Chinese Shar-Pei! Having warned you, I will now say, if you choose your Shar-Pei carefully, there is probably no other breed that will give you more love or more devotion (and sometimes more exasperation!) than a Chinese Shar-Pei.

I don't know how many times I have been asked, "Tell me about the Shar-Pei . . . what are they like?" "Are they good with children?" My answer is always, "You cannot generalize about the Shar-Pei." They have not yet reached that stage of development in their breed history, and indeed, few breeds have. Each Shar-Pei has his own personality and genetic makeup that make him an individual.

Living with a Chinese Shar-Pei

INTELLIGENCE AND INTUITION

Some generalizations, however, I *can* make comfortably: Most Shar-Pei are extremely intelligent. Like other intelligent breeds, they can be taught many things, but they also have a superior understanding of their world and the people in it. I can often communicate with my dogs without saying a word. Language only reinforces what you want them to do or how you would like for them to react.

Chinese Shar-Pei are "people dogs." This I can say unequivocally! They soon become very loyal family members and usually form a strong bond to one member of the family. Wherever you are, that is where your Shar-Pei wants to be. I would be willing to bet that the majority of family Shar-Pei sleep on the bed with "their person." Mine even wait outside the bathroom door. Other breeds (such as the hunting or working dogs) are happiest when in the company of their own species. The Shar-Pei's daily relationships with other household pets may be friendly and she may enjoy all the doggie games, but when a person enters the scene, particularly "her person," the focus of the Shar Pei's attention changes immediately. Perhaps this intense fondness for people is related to pack instinct and deference to the pack leader. I prefer to think they sense our intelligence and the inventiveness and creativity we bring to situations.

Shar-Pei very quickly figure out what pleases their owners and what does not, which brings up another aspect of their intelligence. If you are to own a Shar-Pei, you must be at least as intelligent and intuitive as your dog.

Some Shar-Pei can become very manipulative, and the owner may find him- or herself reinforcing negative or undesirable behavior. For instance, if you are neglecting your dog and not spending enough time with him, you may find that he is doing naughty things to get your attention, much like a child would do.

With Shar-Pei, you *must* always be the "pack leader." You *must* always be the boss! Your relationship with your dog will be a much healthier one. If you are experiencing behavior problems with your Shar-Pei that are beyond your control, seek out a competent trainer or behaviorist before it gets out of hand. Never allow your dog the least bit of aggressive behavior toward you, any member of your family or guests in your home. Keep your dog on a leash and under control when away from your home.

LEAVING YOUR SHAR-PEI ALONE

Because Shar-Pei are "people dogs" and want to be near people, this can pose a problem if you have to work and leave your dog home alone. I personally believe that it is unfair to have a dog who spends eight or more hours alone each day. Whether you have only one Shar-Pei or several, being alone for long periods may bring out some of the less desirable traits for which they were bred. The diligent "guard" may tend to overguard the house, constantly barking, tearing up mail that comes through a door slot,

A DOG'S SENSES

Sight: With their eyes located farther apart than ours, dogs can detect movement at a greater distance than we can, but they can't see as well up close. They can also see better in less light, but can't distinguish many colors.

Sound: Dogs can hear about four times better than we can, and they can hear high-pitched sounds especially well. Their ancestors, the wolves, howled to let other wolves know where they were; our dogs do the same, but they have a wider range of vocalizations, including barks, whimpers, moans and whines.

Smell: A dog's nose is his greatest sensory organ. His sense of smell is so great he can follow a trail that's weeks old, detect odors diluted to one-millionth the concentration we'd need to notice them, even sniff out a person under water!

Taste: Dogs have fewer taste buds than we do, so they're likelier to try anything—and usually do, which is why it's especially important for their owners to monitor their food intake. Dogs are omnivores, which means they eat meat as well as vegetable matter like grasses and weeds.

Touch: Dogs are social animals and love to be petted, groomed and played with.

even chasing imaginary noises or shadows. Getting a companion dog may work, but only if their personalities are compatible; otherwise a serious dogfight may occur when you are not home to break it up. Some owners resort to crating their dogs, but once again, this is hardly humane for extended time periods. So much depends on the individual dog, his temperament and how secure and confident he is. On the other hand, I know quite a few Shar-Pei owners whose Shar-Pei manage quite well when the owners are not home. If your Shar-Pei is to be left alone, you must be especially careful about the dog you choose.

Because of their large muzzles, Shar-Pei can be very messy eaters.

ACTIVITY LEVEL

Some Shar-Pei are very active while others are content to spend most of their day snoozing on the couch (if you allow it). Most seem to require little exercise, which makes them good candidates for apartment living. As with any animal, however, frequent exercise will make for a healthier dog.

CLEANLINESS

Shar-Pei are very clean animals, almost catlike, and are very easily housebroken. The healthy Shar-Pei requires very little grooming except when she is shedding, during which time her short, coarse hair will stick to everything!

Because their muzzles are so large, some Shar-Pei can be very messy eaters and, after a meal, your dog may have food all over her muzzle. If you have more than one Shar-Pei, you will notice that they delight in cleaning each other's muzzles after eating. This is a real ritual in our house. If you only have one dog, you may want to keep her own washcloth handy to clean her muzzle after she has eaten.

Obedience Training Your Shar-Pei

Every Shar-Pei and owner will benefit from some obedience training. You may not be interested in participating in the obedience showring, but the socialization and discipline for both of you will be invaluable, and the Shar-Pei is an ideal candidate. Behavior-modification techniques, whenever necessary, are more easily accomplished through obedience techniques. This breed seems to give respect when respected. Obedience training develops a level of communication between the owner and the dog and through this communication, the dog is better able to find his place within the system, just as he would establish himself within a pack. He is more readily able to understand his owner's expectations. The trained dog will accept a command graciously and go about his business because he is secure. It is easy to develop your Shar-Pei's full potential if you are willing to take the time to educate him.

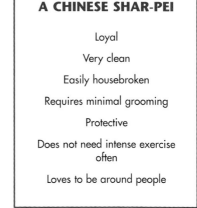

CHARACTERISTICS OF A CHINESE SHAR-PEI

Loyal

Very clean

Easily housebroken

Requires minimal grooming

Protective

Does not need intense exercise often

Loves to be around people

The Shar-Pei is an intelligent animal with a good memory and can be taught to do many things. Many behavioral problems can be avoided simply by making sure he is not bored! Obedience training provides such a constructive outlet. It gives the dog something to do and something to think about. In performing the basics of obedience work, your Shar-Pei is using his mind and working in what is perhaps the most important role a dog can fulfill as stated in the Obedience Regulations, "As a companion to Man."

Enrolling your Shar-Pei in obedience class will keep him occupied and active.

Obedience schools vary in quality and format like any other institution. It is wise to shop around, visit the classes offered in your area, and ask questions about the qualifications of the instructors (don't be afraid to ask for references). Talk with the instructors about your needs and expectations; ask how large the classes are. You are making an investment, and selecting the proper school will reward you with a handsome dividend later on.

MORE INFORMATION ON THE CHINESE SHAR-PEI

NATIONAL BREED CLUB

The Chinese Shar-Pei Club of America
Judy Dorough, Secretary
9806 Mission Blvd.
Riverside, CA 92509

The Chinese Shar-Pei Club of America, Inc., one of the largest breed clubs in the United States, continues to function and act as a voice for the breed through public education, judges' education, rescue networks, breeder referrals, its fifty-six affiliated clubs, veterinary medical research, National and Regional specialties and official publications. It produces a bimonthly magazine, "The Barker," which is filled with information about the Shar-Pei.

BOOKS

Brearley, Joan McDonald. *Book of the Chinese Shar-Pei.* Neptune, N.J.: TFH Publications, Inc., 1991.

Cunliffe, Juliette. *The Chinese Shar-Pei Today.* New York: Howell Book House, 1995.

Gannon, Dee. *The Complete Chinese Shar-Pei.* New York: Howell Book House, 1988.

Redditt, Jo Ann. *Understanding the Chinese Shar-Pei.* Arlington, Va.: Orient Publications, 1989.

MAGAZINES

The Barker
Official Publication of the CSPCA
P. O. Box 6468
Arlington, VA 22206-6468

VIDEO

American Kennel Club. *The Chinese Shar-Pei.*

Living

with a

part two

Chinese Shar-Pei

chapter 4

Bringing Your
Chinese Shar-Pei
Home

Let's assume that you have done your homework in your search for a healthy, well-adjusted Chinese Shar-Pei puppy. You have sought out a reputable breeder, asked all the right questions about the health background of the puppy and her parents, and reached an agreement about the terms of sale. Now you are ready to take your puppy home.

First of all, how old should your puppy be when you take her home? If your puppy will be a pet, it has been proven that the seventh week, and specifically the forty-ninth day, is the perfect time to separate her from her littermates. At this time she will adjust best psychologically to a new environment and has the ability to establish a permanent human-dog relationship. She is gaining confidence and is capable of accepting gentle discipline.

If you choose to bring your puppy home between the eighth and twelfth weeks, keep in mind that this is a fear-imprint period. Traumatic or frightening experiences must be avoided. A second fear-imprint period occurs between six and fourteen months when she is going through the adolescent period. During these periods, be especially gentle and consistent with do's and don'ts.

Necessary Equipment

Before you bring your new puppy home, make sure you have all the necessary equipment at home and in place. She will need food and water bowls, a lightweight buckle collar (no choke chains at this stage, please), a lightweight lead, food, vitamins, safe toys and a crate.

Crate Training

I can hear the gnashing of teeth out there now! A crate? Yes, I firmly believe in crate training for any dog, and puppyhood is the perfect time to teach them (and you) that this is a necessary item. It is not evil. If introduced in the proper way, the crate becomes the puppy's special place. The dog in the wild is a "den animal," preferring to rest and sleep in a dark, quiet place protected from intruders. Although your dog will not live in the wild, there are times when being confined to a crate is for her own safety, much as you and your loved ones are "harnessed" to your seat belts in a car.

There will most likely be times when your dog will have to be crated whether you or she likes it or not. Veterinarians have no choice but to crate animals, and your dog will be ahead of the game if she is accustomed to a crate. The added stress of emotional upset is not needed for a sick animal. If you travel, most hotels will insist (and rightfully so) that your dog be confined to a crate while you are not in your room.

**PUPPY
ESSENTIALS**

Your new
puppy will
need:

food bowl

water bowl

collar

leash

I.D. tag

bed

crate

toys

grooming
supplies

Most likely, your breeder has already introduced your puppy to a crate, but if not, bring the crate home and set it up with comfortable bedding and one or more safe chew toys. Place the crate in a room where the family members will be so that she will not feel isolated—remember, these are social creatures. Do not use newspapers in the bottom of the crate, as she has probably been trained to use them for housebreaking purposes. Do not introduce her to the crate right away, but allow her to investigate. She may voluntarily choose this as her quiet place, especially if she is already familiar with a crate.

Although Chinese Shar-Pei puppies are easily housebroken, a crate makes it just that much easier. A dog will not soil the area to which she is confined if she can possibly help it. However, don't expect miracles, and don't expect an eight- to ten-week-old puppy to go more than a few hours without having to relieve herself.

Before putting your puppy in the crate, remove her collar to keep it *A puppy should be brought home when she's able to establish a close relationship with you and accept gentle discipline.* from getting entangled. Throw a favorite treat into the crate, and if the puppy follows it, close the door. If not, gently place the puppy inside with the treat, tell her she's a "good girl," and close the door.

You can walk just outside the room. If the puppy whines, barks or cries, walk back into the room and shout, "No!" After several attempts at getting your attention, she should settle down and be quiet. Never let a puppy out while she is voicing her objection. This will only reinforce the behavior—that's not the response you want. After she has been quiet for a few minutes, take the puppy out of the crate and immediately praise her and take her outside so that she can relieve herself. Once she has, praise her again, take her back in the house and allow her some time outside the crate.

Repeat this process several times a day, with playtime after each session. Consistency is the key to helping her accept the crate after a few tries. Never use the crate for punishment. She may voluntarily seek it out if she is being reprimanded; at that point, it has become HER place, her haven from your disapproval. Please remember that a puppy should not be confined for long periods; this will create undesired effects and is certainly not the proper use of a crate.

There are many kinds and sizes of crates available. Choose one that will accommodate your puppy into adulthood. It should be at least twenty-four inches tall. Those made of wire provide the best air circulation (the enclosed plastic models can become very hot) and come in collapsible suitcase form for easy transfer to your car.

Housebreaking

If, for some reason, you decide not to purchase a crate, then plan on confining your puppy to one room of your house or apartment, preferably a non-carpeted room such as the kitchen or family room. In this case, you will need one or more gates to keep the puppy confined. This should also be a room where the family members will be a great deal of the time. He should be kept in this room until he is reliably housebroken. If he has free reign of the entire house, he will consider back rooms and the end of a hall as "outside" and a place to relieve himself.

If introduced in the proper way, the crate becomes the puppy's special place.

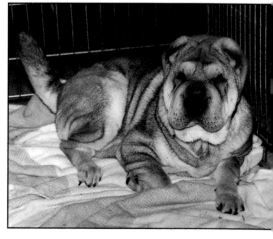

37

Shar-Pei puppies are incredibly easy to housebreak. I have seen puppies who have not yet opened their eyes crawl away from their mother to the opposite side of the whelping box, relieve themselves on newspaper and then crawl back to their mother. When they are able, they will crawl out of the box, complete their business, then crawl back in. Most likely, your seven- or eight-week-old puppy will already be housebroken enough so that you need to take him out only after he eats and on a regular basis in between meals. Accidents, however, will happen. Never hit your puppy or "rub his nose in it." If you can catch him in the act, just say "no" and immediately take him outside. Chastising him after the act never does any good; he will have no idea why you are scolding him.

Identifying Your Puppy

You will want to identify your puppy in some way. Begin by attaching an identification tag to his first lightweight collar. This tag should include your name, address, and phone number, and the name and telephone number of your veterinarian. Puppies are easily distracted, and if your dog accidentally pulls away from you, you have a better chance of recovering him when he is found. As he gets older, more permanent methods of identification, such as a tattoo or microchip implantation, would be better, especially if your Shar-Pei tends to pull out of his collar. Discuss these alternatives with your veterinarian. Tattoos are usually placed on the inside of the leg, and the number is registered with one of the national

---

HOUSEHOLD DANGERS

Curious puppies and inquisitive dogs get into trouble not because they are bad, but simply because they want to investigate the world around them. It's our job to protect our dogs from harmful substances, like the following:

IN THE HOUSE

cleaners, especially pine oil

perfumes, colognes, aftershaves

medications, vitamins

office and craft supplies

electric cords

chicken or turkey bones

chocolate

some house and garden plants, like ivy, oleander and poinsettia

IN THE GARAGE

antifreeze

garden supplies, like snail and slug bait, pesticides, fertilizers, mouse and rat poisons

---

registries. Microchip implantation is becoming more popular and has just been approved by the American Kennel Club as a proper means of identification. Many animal shelters now have microchip scanners that will help identify your dog if he is rescued.

Chewing

By the time you bring your puppy home, he will have a full complement of deciduous, or "puppy," teeth. These teeth are very sharp and will inflict puncture wounds if you allow him to play too roughly. When they have served their purpose, around the time when the puppy is four to five months old, a more substantial set of teeth is necessary. This new set of forty-two permanent teeth begins to come in and pushes out the puppy teeth. During the time that your puppy is getting his new teeth, he will want to chew quite a bit, and some dogs remain "chewers" well into adulthood.

This is a good time to mention that Shar-Pei seem to use their mouths to show their affection to their human counterparts. Don't be alarmed if your Shar-Pei puppy wants to take your hand or arm in his mouth; this seems to be one way they express, "I love

Puppies should have plenty of safe toys to chew on.

you." Puppies, however, can sometimes go too far and bite too hard. Just say "No" and show them a more appropriate way to express their adoration.

You should have several chew toys for your puppy. If he has his own toys, he is much less likely to chew on furniture, shoes, and so on. In my opinion, it is best to avoid those items that can be ingested in large chunks such as rawhide, cow hooves or pigs' ears, which are sold in pet shops. Rawhide can cause choking or intestinal blockage; cow hooves come off in slivers and can cause damage to the stomach and intestines, as can dried pigs' ears. Yes, dogs love all of them, but they are not what can best satisfy your puppy's chewing needs. I recommend hard rubber toys or sterilized bones that are hard but do not break off in chips. As the puppy gets his permanent teeth and his chewing power increases, you may want to remove the hard rubber items, especially if he begins to chew them apart into small pieces. If unwanted chewing is a problem, try spraying Bitter Apple (available in pet stores) on those things you do not want your puppy to chew.

Leash Training

Take your puppy for frequent walks to introduce him to the outside world, the leash and regular exercise. Make it fun. If he sits and refuses to budge, squat down to his level and cajole him to come in to you. Always use his name, and don't fight for control. Work slowly and allow the pup time to understand and accept the idea of your leadership. As he becomes familiar with walking on-lead, take him a bit farther out into the world. Let him experience short walks at first, then make your walks longer. You, too, will benefit from the exercise. See chapter 8 for more information about leash-training your puppy.

"Puppy-proofing" Your Home

Just as you would "baby-proof" your home if you have a toddler, you will want to "puppy-proof" all the rooms to which your puppy will have access. Make sure there is nothing harmful the puppy can chew, such as electrical cords, plants or knickknacks on low tables. Where do you keep your household cleaners or medications? Toxic materials usually stored outside must be put where the puppy cannot get them. This includes things like gasoline for the lawn mower, antifreeze (which is extremely toxic, and dogs seem to like the taste), insecticides, fungicides, fertilizers, and so on. Try to think like a puppy who, with a fiendish look in his eye, will say, "What can I get into now?" Remove it before it can cause harm.

Bringing Home an Adult Dog

If your new Shar-Pei is an adult dog, you will have a completely different set of considerations to help him adapt to his new environment. Puppies are usually very adaptable and adjust to new environments easily. The adult dog has a history and will most likely be more cautious and possibly more fearful, depending on his background.

As you would do for a puppy, make sure he encounters as little stress as possible. Allow him to investigate his surroundings, and occasionally call him over and praise him for coming. He will need lots of approval. Walk the adult dog often, just as you would your puppy. This acquaints him with his outside surroundings and allows him to set his boundaries mentally.

Don't be surprised if he relieves himself inside. This is a dog's way of "marking" his new territory. If it happens, it will most likely happen only once. Clean it up and try not to scold him. If he repeats the behavior, then simply say "No" and take him outside until he relieves himself; then praise him and bring him back inside.

Make sure you puppy-proof your home so that curious puppies can't get hurt.

If you are bringing him to a home where there are small children, do not allow them to rush at the dog. Instead have your first introductions take place in as quiet and calm a manner as possible.

The Multiple-Dog Home

In our discussion thus far, we have assumed that the new Shar-Pei is coming home to a house with no other

41

animals. If you have other pets, make sure they are confined until your Shar-Pei (puppy or adult) has had time to acquaint herself with this new place. After all, your home is your first dog's territory, and you are bringing a stranger into *his* place. Using puppy gates allows two dogs to become acquainted without having access to each other. If you are introducing a puppy to an adult dog, hold the puppy in your lap and let the adult dog sniff her. Most (and I emphasize *most*) adult dogs will not harm puppies. Until you are comfortable that the older dog has accepted the new puppy, always supervise the situation.

Having a multiple-dog home can be wonderful, but make sure the animals are properly introduced.

With two adult dogs, you will have to be even more careful. Dogs are territorial, and the first dog may resent the intruder even if you have accepted her. A great deal depends upon the personality and temperaments of the individual dogs, and it is better to be careful and plan ahead. It is best to introduce two adult dogs on neutral territory outside the home, then perhaps bring the two into the house together. Or keep them separated until they have at least become acquainted through a gate. Nothing is worse than a dogfight, and anticipating a problem is half the battle of solving it.

chapter 5

Feeding
Your
Chinese Shar-Pei

It's nice to see the pet super-stores coming to shopping centers all over the country. You have only to visit one of these stores to see the great variety of dog foods available. Understandably, with so much variety, new owners are sometimes confused about what type of food is best for their dog. Many dog foods contain high percentages of protein, and these are fine for the very active or working dogs, but the Shar-Pei leads a fairly

sedentary life and requires far less protein in his diet. However, your Shar-Pei will need all those nutrients necessary for a well-balanced diet to help him grow and maintain good health.

The amount you should feed your Shar-Pei will vary with each dog. Factors to take into consideration are his age, his activity level, his physical condition and the time of the year. Dogs seem to need more food in the winter (especially if they spend a lot of time outdoors) than in the summer. The Shar-Pei puppy weighing ten to twenty pounds needs approximately 700 to 1,200 calories per day; the twenty- to thirty-pound puppy needs 1,200 to 1,400 calories per day; and the thirty- to fifty-pound dog needs 930 to 2,000 calories per day. All these figures will be slightly less in summer and slightly higher in winter. An average pound of dry dog food contains 1,550 to 1,600 calories, or 300 to 400 per cup. Check the information on the side of the bag of food for caloric content.

Dog food manufacturers spend a great deal of money on research and development in an attempt to produce dog food that is nutritional. While you can cook for your dog, it would be difficult (but not impossible) for you to achieve the same balance of the proper ingredients in the proper proportions necessary for your dog. Unless you understand the nutritional requirements of your dog, it is far better to choose a balanced, commercially prepared, name-brand dog food and stick to it.

Puppies grow very quickly and may need extra protein in their diet.

By the time you bring your puppy home, he is perfectly capable of eating commercially prepared dry dog food. There are many good ones on the market, but there are a few rules to remember about what you feed your Shar-Pei.

First, select a well-balanced dry dog food that contains less than 17 percent protein (14 percent to 16 percent for adults). Some Shar-Pei cannot process high levels of protein adequately, and this results in a protein buildup in the kidneys. While protein is necessary to build muscle, high levels of protein are not necessary for healthy physical or mental development in the Shar-Pei—and can be damaging.

Shar-Pei puppies grow very fast, and most reach their adult height by six months of age. They may need a little more food from time to time, but begin by offering one cup of moistened kibble to which you have added one-fourth to one-half a can of canned dog food for palatability. Until a puppy is about six months old, you may want to mix approximately two tablespoons of cottage cheese or yogurt with their soaked dry food once a day. These dairy products are a natural source of extra protein as well as calcium for healthy teeth and bones. It is unwise, however, to use calcium supplements unless prescribed by a veterinarian. A well-balanced diet usually provides adequate calcium intake, and excess amounts cannot be used by the body and can cause kidney or bladder stones or painful calcified joints. The addition of supplements should be kept to a minimum as an excess or imbalance of vitamins and minerals can be dangerous. An excess of vitamin D or vitamin A can be toxic. If your veterinarian feels there is a need for additional supplements, follow his or her advice.

HOW MANY MEALS A DAY?

Individual dogs vary in how much they should eat to maintain a desired body weight—not too fat, but not too thin. Puppies need several meals a day, while older dogs may need only one. Determine how much food keeps your adult dog looking and feeling her best. Then decide how many meals you want to feed with that amount. Like us, most dogs love to eat, and offering two meals a day is more enjoyable for them. If you're worried about overfeeding, make sure you measure correctly and abstain from adding tidbits to the meals.

Whether you feed one or two meals, only leave your dog's food out for the amount of time it takes her to eat it—10 minutes, for example. Freefeeding (when food is available any time) and leisurely meals encourage picky eating. Don't worry if your dog doesn't finish all her dinner in the allotted time. She'll learn she should.

Vitamin C

There is one vitamin supplement that I do use and recommend for at least the first year of life: Vitamin C (ascorbic acid). Vitamin C helps to build immunity and promotes the production of collagen. I have seen Shar-Pei puppies with splayed feet, once placed on daily doses of vitamin C, come up on their toes within a two-week period and develop the tight, compact feet called for in the standard. In my opinion, this was what was needed in the production of collagen to strengthen the tendons and ligaments of the toes.

Veterinarians not acquainted with the benefits of vitamin C will tell you that dogs produce their own vitamin C and do not need these supplements. Your Shar-Pei, however, has a better way of telling you whether he is producing enough of this essential vitamin. If your dog does not need it or is getting too much, he will develop loose stools. How much should you start with?

With puppies over six weeks, you can begin with one 250 milligrams children's chewable tablet. (Vitamin C is ascorbic acid and is more easily digested in the coated children's chewable version. In the uncoated form, it can cause too much acid in the stomach.) Or, an even better powdered form of vitamin C, sodium ascorbic, can be purchased from a health food store. It is less expensive in this form, and one-quarter teaspoon contains 1,000 milligrams (1 gram) and can be added to your dog's food. Gradually increase the dosage every two to three weeks until, around the age of six months, the dog is taking 1,500 milligrams. If the dog develops loose stools at any time, back off on the dosage. When (and if) this happens, your Shar-Pei has probably reached his individual level needed for producing immunity.

Not all of my Shar-Pei needed vitamin C (I could tell because the minimum dosage caused loose stools), but invariably those were the dogs with very healthy coats, and good bone and muscle development. I strongly recommend the book *How to Have a Healthier Dog*, by Dr. Wendell Belfield, for a complete explanation of the benefits and usage of vitamin C. He also dispels some of the myths about this important supplement. After one year of age, the dog does not have as great a need for vitamin C unless he has allergies. Later in life, failing organs can sometimes be rejuvenated with vitamin C and help the older dog to live a few more good years. It can also help the dog who has been under stress, and it can aid in the recuperation from an illness or surgery.

Allergies

It is wise to avoid any dog food containing soy products. This is not a hard-and-fast rule because soy can be an important source of protein for both humans and animals, but some Shar-Pei are allergic to soy products. If your dog develops allergic symptoms such as itching, vomiting or chronic loose stools, check his dog food for soy products.

Should your dog become allergic to any of the ingredients in his food, I have discovered that there is hope. Ming, an apparently healthy, six-year-old Shar-Pei developed chronic diarrhea. Her owner first had her tested for intestinal parasites—negative. She was wormed anyway, just to make sure—still the diarrhea continued. Following the vet's suggestion, the owner first tried feeding her rice and beef, then rice and chicken—no improvement. All the tests conducted by the veterinarian came back negative and left everyone scratching their heads. No one could figure out what was wrong with Ming.

TO SUPPLEMENT OR NOT TO SUPPLEMENT?

If you're feeding your dog a diet that's correct for her developmental stage and she's alert, healthy-looking and neither over- nor underweight, you don't need to add supplements. These include table scraps as well as vitamins and minerals. In fact, a growing puppy is in danger of developing musculoskeletal disorders by oversupplementation. If you have any concerns about the nutritional quality of the food you're feeding, discuss them with your veterinarian.

This robust forty-five-pound Shar-Pei was soon reduced to a twenty-eight-pound dog who was fast fading. Then her owner heard about the "Elisa" test and asked her vet to try it. This is a simple blood test that will identify those foods to which your dog is allergic. The results of the test indicated that Ming was allergic to two of the most common ingredients in dog foods: corn and rice. Her owner was given a list of about thirty foods that were high on the "no-no" list, while others were not as offensive to Ming's allergies. Mind you, this was a dog who had never exhibited any indication of allergies before six years of age. Her owner fed her potatoes, bread and ground beef, all of which were non-allergic according to the test, for a month. The diarrhea disappeared immediately, and she gradually gained back all the weight she had lost. Today, she is nine years old, and although she occasionally has a bout of diarrhea, it is quickly arrested. Her owner searched for food to which Ming was not allergic and found several sources, which included wheat, barley, duck, rabbit and venison. All these special diets are available through your veterinarian.

Preparing Your Shar-Pei's Food

Always (and I can't emphasize this enough), always soak your dog's dry food in water for at least thirty minutes before feeding. If you place equal amounts of water and dry food in a bowl, you will notice that the food expands—which is exactly what happens when you feed your dog dry food and he drinks water: The food expands in the stomach, which can cause gas buildup. While no one can give a definitive answer as to why a dog "bloats," one of the theories that makes sense to me is the constant expanding and contracting of the stomach that occurs in a dog who is always fed dry dog food. (You can read more about bloat in chapter 7.)

An older dog requires less protein and fewer calories than he did when he was younger.

For this reason, I do not approve of "free feeding" or leaving dry food in your dog's bowl and allowing him to eat anytime (or as much) as he wishes. Feed your young dog smaller amounts of soaked food at least three times a day until he is three months old, then twice a day for the rest of his life. Many dogs, including the Shar-Pei, will throw up yellow bile if their stomachs are empty for long periods. Feeding them more often will help eliminate this problem.

Appetite Loss

Once in a while, with no explanation, a dog will "go off his feed." If you can find no health reason for this decrease in appetite, just lower the amount you offer him for a while and wait for his appetite to come back. Perhaps you are feeding him too much. Offering him tasty incentives in the form of people food will only spoil him, and you will most likely find it even more difficult to get him back on his routine. An experienced breeder once told me that periodically, dogs in the wild will voluntarily fast for a day and consequently, she, too, would skip feedings for a twenty-four-hour period at least once a month. Her dogs always appeared healthy, and periodic fasting seems to be preferable to having an overweight dog. If your "picky eater" refuses his food, remove the dish and wait an hour or two, or even until his next regular meal. Unless a dog is ill, he will eventually eat.

Never feed your dog after he has been playing or vigorously exercising. Let him drink, then rest before eating. Likewise, do not allow your dog to become very active after a meal, as this can cause him to vomit and/or bloat.

Cooking for Your Shar-Pei

If you are the type who would like to cook for your dog, there are many specialty cookbooks on the

---

HOW TO READ THE DOG FOOD LABEL

With so many choices on the market, how can you be sure you are feeding the right food for your dog? The information is all there on the label—if you know what you're looking for.

Look for the nutritional claim right up top. Is the food "100% nutritionally complete"? If so, it's for nearly all life stages; "growth and maintenance," on the other hand, is for early development; puppy foods are marked as such, as are foods for senior dogs.

Ingredients are listed in descending order by weight. The first three or four ingredients will tell you the bulk of what the food contains. Look for the highest-quality ingredients, like meats and grains, to be among them.

The Guaranteed Analysis tells you what levels of protein, fat, fiber and moisture are in the food, in that order. While these numbers are meaningful, they won't tell you much about the quality of the food. Nutritional value is in the dry matter, not the moisture content.

In many ways, seeing is believing. If your dog has bright eyes, a shiny coat, a good appetite and a good energy level, chances are his diet's fine. Your dog's breeder and your veterinarian are good sources of advice if you're still confused.

market that can explain how to prepare a well-balanced diet for him. From time to time I have tried this, especially when I had a dog who was suffering from allergies. If you have the time to cook for your dog, start with brown rice, to which you might add carrots, celery and broccoli along with chicken, beef, lamb or fish, plus a daily multivitamin supplement recommended by your veterinarian. Completely avoid the skin of chicken or fish because these contain too much fat and will cause loose stools. Once when I thought our Shar-Pei should share in Thanksgiving dinner, I fed him turkey skin. Both he and I were very sorry a short time later!

Feeding Scraps

Although it is difficult to ignore those begging eyes, it is best to avoid giving your dog table scraps. Look at the situation realistically. Your dog's diet is nutritional, well-balanced and sufficient for his growth and development. What more does he need? Perhaps you have given in to those pleading eyes once too often and taught him that it's okay to beg. Let's put the shoe on the other foot (or paw, if you will). How do you think he would respond if you sat by his bowl while he was eating and whined and begged for just a tidbit from his bowl? You would probably get nipped on the nose and justly so! His response would be appropriate for a dog; by feeding him from the table, you are teaching him to behave inappropriately.

There are some people foods that can be very upsetting to your dog's digestive system, or even toxic. These include spicy and heavily salted foods. Chocolate can be toxic to some dogs, and recently, onions have been added to the "avoid at all costs" list as possibly harmful.

Treats

Keep a container of dog biscuits on hand to reinforce good behavior. My canister sits on the kitchen counter filled with small snack bones that I give out sparingly when one of my dogs completes a command. For instance, when I leave the house to run an errand, I command each dog to "go in your crate" for their own safety. Once they are in, I praise them and give them each a dog biscuit. If they are outside and I want them to come in, I give them a biscuit when they respond immediately. Once you have established a behavior pattern that teaches your dog to respond to your command and receive a treat for responding, then you can decide whether you always want to reinforce the behavior with a treat. Otherwise, you may find that your intelligent Shar-Pei is manipulating you. You think, "Oh, what a good dog! He is doing everything I want him to do. Give him a treat!" when actually he is performing certain behaviors *only* to get a treat, not necessarily to please you or because he is well-trained.

For example, let's say that your dog gets a treat when he barks at the back door to let you know he needs to go out and relieve himself . . . he goes . . . comes right back in and gets a treat for doing so. Soon, he may decide that if he is going to get a treat every time he does this, he will do it more often. Bark! Bark! If your dog really craves his treats, he may be performing this act to get the treat and not because he needs to go out and relieve himself. If you see this type of behavior developing, then give him a treat every other time he goes out—or only occasionally. Because of the breed's intelligence, this type of behavior in the Shar-Pei is not uncommon.

TYPES OF FOODS/TREATS

There are three types of commercially available dog food—dry, canned and semimoist—and a huge assortment of treats (lucky dogs!) to feed your dog. Which should you choose?

Dry and canned foods contain similar ingredients. The primary difference between them is their moisture content. The moisture is not just water. It's blood and broth, too, the very things that dogs adore. So while canned food is more palatable, dry food is more economical, convenient and effective in controlling tartar buildup. Most owners feed a 25% canned/75% dry diet to give their dogs the benefit of both. Just be sure your dog is getting the nutrition he needs (you and your veterinarian can determine this).

Semimoist foods have the flavor dogs love and the convenience owners want. However, they tend to contain excessive amounts of artificial colors and preservatives.

Dog treats come in every size, shape and flavor imaginable, from organic cookies shaped like postmen to beefy chew sticks. Dogs seem to love them all, so enjoy the variety. Just be sure not to overindulge your dog. Factor treats into her regular meal sizes.

Weight Problems

Just as some people do, some Shar-Pei seem to convert every morsel of food into fat. A dog's caloric intake should be dictated by his metabolism and the amount of energy he expends. The nervous dog or the highly energetic dog will rarely be overweight, but the sedentary dog or "couch potato," which some Shar-Pei are, may have a tendency to gain weight. Giving the overweight dog smaller amounts of food several times a day will keep him happier and more satisfied than if he is fed only one or two meals. This also prevents his stomach from becoming too empty. When placing your dog on a diet, check the calorie content per pound or cup of dog food on the side of the bag. Increase the amount of exercise for the overweight dog—for instance, by taking him for long walks. You, too, will benefit from this.

As the older dog's system slows down, he won't need as many calories as he did when he was younger. After age six or seven years, you will most certainly want to reduce the protein and fat levels in your Shar-Pei's food because of the threat of kidney disease. Continued exercise can help prevent obesity and can delay or alleviate arthritic conditions. As he ages, you may want to supplement his diet with vitamin E (400 IU per day), which can be helpful in maintaining good circulation and healthy skin.

If, or when, you change your dog's diet, do it gradually by adding some of the new food to the old over a period of at least a week until you have replaced the old food. Drastic changes can cause digestive upsets such as vomiting or diarrhea. Constipation may be caused by an imbalanced diet, an irregular diet or not enough water or roughage in the diet. Feeding foods such as small amounts of beef, lamb or chicken liver, or wheat or oat bran will loosen the stools and help relieve constipation.

chapter 6

Grooming
Your
Chinese Shar-Pei

A "Wash and Wear" Dog

This is the easy part. The healthy Shar-Pei is a clean, easy-care, "wash and wear" dog. Some Shar-Pei may occasionally have skin problems, which will need a little more care, but for

the most part your dog will need only an occasional bath. Some Shar-Pei seem to impart a natural "perfume" that is pleasant smelling; these dogs need bathing even less often. Too many baths can dry out the skin. In between baths, an occasional rubdown with a damp cloth will keep the surface of his coat, underbelly and face clean.

Make bath time a pleasant time, gently rubbing and talking to your dog and telling him what a "good boy (or girl)" he or she is. Although most Shar-Pei hate water, they can learn to enjoy baths if they don't become stressful situations.

Allowing water to get in the ears can lead to an ear infection. Be very careful not to let the water get above the neck. By placing cotton or lamb's wool (available at your drugstore) in her ears during the bath, you will be sure that no water gets in.

There are so many types of dog shampoos on the market, it is difficult to know just what is best for your dog. The varieties are endless: herbal, cream, mink oil, protein degreasing, moisturizing pearls, flea and tick formulas, ad infinitum. Because the Shar-Pei has a harsh coat, you do not want to use a softening agent in your shampoo or a cream rinse *unless* you are extremely allergic to their harsh coats. Many owners complain, "My dog makes me break out! If I hug him, my arms have little red bumps!" You can lessen this allergic reaction by using a softening agent in his rinse water.

His harsher coat can be sacrificed for your comfort unless you have a show dog who will be judged on the harshness of his coat.

Some Shar-Pei with dry skin will have dandruff, which shows up more on the black dogs. Bathing these dogs more often will

Shar-Pei have short coarse coats that do not need considerable brushing unless they are shedding.

only dry out their skin even more. Instead, use one of the non-drying dermatology spray products between baths. For the dog who has no skin problems, a non-drying type of canine shampoo (never use detergents) should be used, and always rinse well. If you think you have rinsed enough, rinse a little more. Pull the wrinkles apart and rinse in between so that you don't leave any soap residue that can cause irritation and itching. For the dog who has experienced skin problems, you will want to use an antibacterial shampoo and perhaps an antiallergic rinse or spray.

Shedding

Shar-Pei don't really need routine brushing except when they are shedding, but it does help to produce healthy circulation in the skin and remove dead hair. Unlike many other breeds, Shar-Pei have no undercoat that needs removing. When they shed hair, it naturally falls out instead of remaining next to the skin. A good natural-bristle brush will do for day-to-day brushing.

While your Shar-Pei is shedding, you may want to insist she stay off the couch.

Shar-Pei usually shed their coats twice a year. Every dog has his own cycle and usually sheds once between early spring and early summer and again between Thanksgiving and New Year. During these times, you can run your hand across the back of the dog and come up with a handful of hair. These shedding cycles are referred to by breeders as "blowing their coat." There are several products on the market that will help remove this dead hair: rubber mitts, which have rubber "teeth" (grooming gloves); metal currying brushes ("slickers"—sometimes too abrasive on the very short coats); and (the product I like best) the "shedding blade," a long stainless steel blade with teeth that can be looped around and secured to form a handle. When using one of these blades, it is best to use it outside as it will pull out copious amounts of shedding hair. The shedding cycle of the Shar-Pei may seem endless, sometimes lasting for a month, but when completed, the dog has a beautiful new coat. During these cycles, you may want to insist that your dog stay off the furniture because their short bristly hair sticks in upholstery and is very difficult to remove. (Yes, my dogs do have access to my furniture as well as to my bed.)

Toenails

Another generalization I can make about this breed is that, almost universally, they resent anyone doing anything with their feet, and toenail trimming can be an unpleasant chore. However, it is necessary. You must begin when they are very young and do it on a regular basis.

GROOMING
TOOLS

pin brush

slicker brush

flea comb

towel

mat rake

grooming
glove

scissors

nail
clippers

tooth-
cleaning
equipment

shampoo

conditioner

clippers

With young puppies, their nails are still small enough for you to use regular toenail snips, but as they mature, their nails will get large and thick, and you will have to invest in a good pair of guillotine toenail clippers. I have devised my own technique that works best for me, but it takes two people—one to hold the head and comfort the dog while I hold the dog between my knees, lift the leg and snip away. I have tried every method with my Shar-Pei, and they seem to object the least to this one. You don't want this chore to turn into a struggling match. The dog feels more comfortable because he is standing. By forcing him to lie down for this procedure, you are only causing more stress. If all else fails, you can take your dog to the vet's office for toenail clipping, but this can lead to the dog hating vet visits. It's best to let your dog know who's boss and insist that he cooperate with you even if you have to pull out the muzzle and use it.

If you trim the nails on a regular basis (at least every two weeks), you will have to snip off only the end of the toenail (about one-eighth inch at a time). This will keep the toenails short enough, but if too much time elapses between trims, the nails will become too long and the "quick" (the blood supply to the nail) will grow along with the nail. Trimming frequently inhibits the growth of the quick. If at all possible, cut the dog's nails outside on a sunny day. This way, you can see the quick and avoid cutting the nail too close (unless your dog has very black nails, but even then the sunlight will help reveal the quick). Keep a styptic powder on hand in case you accidentally cut into the quick. A little of this powder placed on the end of the nail will stop the bleeding, though your dog will most definitely let you know that you have erred.

Don't forget the dewclaw, if your Shar-Pei still has two (or more). These rudimentary "thumbs" are located farther up on the inside of the leg just above the foot. If your dog was born with them, your breeder may have removed them shortly after birth. Check both front and hind legs for dewclaws. While most Shar-Pei do not have rear dewclaws, some are born with them. They should have been removed by the breeder but may still be present. If neglected, dewclaws can continue to grow and curve into the leg, and

Chewing on hard toys will help keep your Shar-Pei's teeth clean.

becomevery painful and possibly infected. If this happens, your veterinarian will need to remove them surgically. Careful maintenance will avoid this.

Tooth Care

The practice of good preventive dentistry is just as important for your Shar-Pei as it is for you, and dogs are susceptible to the same dental diseases as humans: cavities, tartar or plaque buildup, abscesses and gum disease. Tartar and plaque buildup can lead to gingivitis, the swelling and inflammation of the gums, which, if left untreated, can result in infections and even tooth loss. Much of this can be prevented with the proper care.

Many veterinarians recommend regular toothbrushing for dogs. This is best begun at an early age, and there are even canine toothpaste products. However, if you notice tartar building up on your dog's teeth, you may use a homemade paste of bicarbonate of soda and peroxide. Place this paste on a piece of gauze and rub it on the teeth (gauze provides more abrasiveness than a toothbrush). You can sometimes scrape away plaque with your fingernail.

Shar-Pei are clean, easy to groom dogs; some even seem to impart a natural perfume.

Trying to determine whether your Shar-Pei has any gum problems may be difficult not only for you but also for the veterinarian, because many Shar-Pei have black gums. Nevertheless, a good teeth cleaning every year should ensure that your dog has healthy teeth. Most vets will insist that the dog be anesthetized for this procedure.

Access to safe chew toys will also help keep his teeth clean. By safe, I mean toys that will not break and splinter—for example, hard, sterilized bones, or nylon bones, which become rough and abrasive after a little chewing and help to clean the teeth.

If you notice that your dog has particularly bad breath, ask the veterinarian to check the teeth. He may have an abscessed tooth, tonsillitis or any one of several other health problems causing the foul odor.

Eye Care

Eye care and the problems connected with eye disease are discussed more extensively in the chapter 7, but for the vast majority of Shar-Pei, you will need to do very little in the way of eye health care. Only occasionally, you may see a little matter exuding from the eyes—particularly in the morning when the dog wakes up. Simply clean this with a damp soft cloth. Pollen season can cause some running of the eyes, and the same procedure applies.

Ear Care

Routine ear cleaning is necessary only every couple of weeks unless your Shar-Pei has very small ear canals or excess wax buildup. Clean the outer ear with a damp cotton ball dipped in a little alcohol or baby oil. A cotton swab dipped in the same solutions can be used to clean only the outer

Gently clean your Shar-Pei's ears every couple of weeks.

portion of the ear canal, carefully removing the wax. Do not push the swab too far into the ear canal—this can damage the ear. If you notice a foul odor or any sort of drainage (pus) coming from the ear canal, this usually indicates an ear infection. See your veterinarian for the proper medication. A very dark or black residue in the ears can indicate the presence of parasitic ear mites. Very tight or small ear canals may lead to chronic yeast infections. Again, check this out with your veterinarian.

chapter 7

Keeping Your
Chinese Shar-Pei
Healthy

Your dog is a living, breathing animal and as such is subject to a myriad of diseases, just as humans are. Everyone who purchases a puppy hopes that he will live a long, full, healthy life, but life doesn't offer any guarantees, and it will be your responsibility to help keep your dog as healthy as possible. Just as it is important for you to have periodic medical checkups, so it is for your dog. The first time you see a vet should be within forty-eight hours of purchasing you new puppy. This is an "insurance policy" of sorts to assure you and your breeder that the puppy is healthy at the time of purchase and has no obvious health problems.

Choosing a Veterinarian

Before choosing a veterinarian, make a few calls to be sure you have chosen the best health care provider possible for your puppy. A local Chinese Shar-Pei Club can recommend a veterinarian familiar with the treatment of Shar-Pei. Since the breed is fairly new to the United States, not all veterinarians are familiar with the breed or some of the more recent treatments for medical problems specific to the Shar-Pei. If you cannot get a referral from another Shar-Pei owner, then start by calling some veterinarians close to you and asking a few questions such as: Have you treated any Shar-Pei in your practice? How many? Do you do eyetacking or entropion surgery? Are you familiar with some of the problems encountered by this breed? Educate yourself so that you can intelligently discuss your dog and what is expected of a client-vet relationship.

Your first trip to the vet is a very important one. If your puppy (or dog) is a calm, well-socialized dog who loves everyone, it is not likely you will encounter any problems. If he is a little timid and fearful, however, it is most important that you reassure him and that the veterinarian treat him gently. This first visit is not the time for any elective procedures such as toenail clipping. It should be a pleasant visit with little or no stress. If for any reason you feel the veterinarian is being too rough or too forceful in his or her handling of your animal, you must take charge, thank him or her, and walk out. You are the client, and you must make any final decisions concerning your puppy's well-being. A bad experience on your first visit can set up a pattern of behavior that can last a lifetime—or worse.

Vaccinations

When you purchase your Shar-Pei puppy, she should have already had at least one vaccination for parvovirus and distemper. Your breeder should provide you with information on the types of vaccines your Shar-Pei has had and the dates they were given. It will be up to you to continue her inoculation schedule.

Normal, healthy puppies should begin their immunization schedule at approximately six weeks of age. Boosters should be given once a year except for dogs attending dog shows. Because of the increased exposure to canine illnesses, these dogs should receive boosters at least every six months.

It is rare, but not unheard of, for a puppy to have a reaction to a vaccination. These reactions can range from mild to severe; severe ones will usually occur within a half hour after injection. Some veterinarians will ask you to wait in the office a short time to make sure your puppy is not going to have a reaction. Watch your puppy for twelve to twenty-four hours after an injection. If you note lethargy, shaking, fever or any unusual symptoms, contact your veterinarian. Many breeders prefer to give the parvovirus and distemper combinations separately at least a week apart. In addition to giving the parvo and distemper separately, most Shar-Pei breeders prefer to give the rabies injections on still another office visit. No matter what schedule you choose to follow, it is extremely important that your Shar-Pei be protected from the most common viral and bacterial diseases:

Take your puppy to the vet within two days of bringing her home.

Canine distemper is a very serious canine viral disease that usually affects the gastrointestinal system, the respiratory system and the nervous system. It can occur at any age but is most devastating to very young and very old dogs. A thick, yellowish discharge from the nose, matter in the eyes, fever and refusal to eat are some of the symptoms. Pneumonia can develop, and encephalitis can result from the high fever, which sometimes leads to brain damage.

Canine coronavirus infection is a highly contagious disease affecting the gastrointestinal tract. While not usually as virulent, the symptoms are similar to those of parvovirus: a high fever, vomiting and an orange/

yellowish diarrhea. This is especially serious in young puppies because of the danger of dehydration.

Bordetella is one of the major bacterial components of a disease complex known as "kennel cough" or infectious tracheobronchitis. This is an acute respiratory disease in dogs, which manifests as a dry, non-productive cough. It can then be further complicated by bacterial infection with agents such as Bordetella and the mycoplasmas. It is advisable to protect your dog with a vaccination at least two weeks before he is exposed to other dogs either in a kennel/boarding situation or at a dog show, as Bordetella is highly contagious.

Canine leptospirosis is a bacterial infection that may lead to permanent kidney damage. It is easily spread to other pets and to humans.

Canine parainfluenza is another cause of kennel cough. Although it is often a mild respiratory infection in otherwise healthy dogs, it can be severe in puppies or weaker dogs.

Canine parvovirus is an intestinal viral disease that first appeared in 1977. Symptoms include a high fever, severe depression, vomiting

> ### YOUR PUPPY'S VACCINES
>
> Vaccines are given to prevent your dog from getting an infectious disease like canine distemper or rabies. Vaccines are the ultimate preventive medicine: they're given before your dog ever gets the disease so as to protect him from the disease. That's why it is necessary for your dog to be vaccinated routinely. Puppy vaccines start at eight weeks of age for the five-in-one DHLPP vaccine and are given every three to four weeks until the puppy is sixteen months old. Your veterinarian will put your puppy on a proper schedule and will remind you when to bring in your dog for shots.

and loose, bloody stools. It is particularly lethal to very young dogs and older dogs. Dehydration may occur due to the vomiting and diarrhea. Once a dog has contracted parvo, supportive therapy of fluids and electrolytes is necessary. As veterinarians become more knowledgeable about the disease, it is becoming more treatable but still requires very intensive treatment.

Lyme disease is a bacterial disease caused by a spirochete (*Borrelia Burgdorferi*) and is thought to be spread through direct contact with ticks (especially the deer tick, which is so small it often goes undetected).

Arthritis-like symptoms may occur and one of the first symptoms in the dog is lameness, which if untreated subsides but returns and gets progressively worse. In humans, the disease usually begins with a rash and mild, flulike symptoms. The dog may have had a rash that went undetected because of his coat. If treated early with antibiotics, most patients will recover without complications, but the disease is often either undiagnosed or misdiagnosed. Always check yourself and your dog for ticks after an outing in grass or woods. In case of illness, keep any ticks found imbedded in the skin in alcohol for further examination.

Rabies is one of the world's most publicized and feared diseases and is almost always fatal to both animals and humans. The rabies virus attacks the central nervous system and is transmitted through the bite of an infected animal. Because it is probably the most serious disease that can be spread to man from an infected animal, all states require that your dog be vaccinated against rabies. State laws vary, but the usual required age for vaccination is four to six months. Even though your dog is confined to your home and yard, this does not mean that she cannot contract rabies from a wild animal or roaming domesticated animal. The incidence of rabies is increasing in skunks, raccoons, foxes, bats and woodchucks (groundhogs), and it is not uncommon for one of these animals to appear in a suburban backyard.

A FIRST-AID KIT

Keep a canine first-aid kit on hand for general care and emergencies. Check it periodically to make sure liquids haven't spilled or dried up, and replace medications and materials after they're used. Your kit should include:

Activated charcoal tablets

Adhesive tape
(1 and 2 inches wide)

Antibacterial ointment
(for skin and eyes)

Aspirin (buffered or enteric coated, *not* Ibuprofen)

Bandages: Gauze rolls (1 and 2 inches wide) and dressing pads

Cotton balls

Diarrhea medicine

Dosing syringe

Hydrogen peroxide (3%)

Petroleum jelly

Rectal thermometer

Rubber gloves

Rubbing alcohol

Scissors

Tourniquet

Towel

Tweezers

If your dog is bitten by any other animal, either wild or domesticated, it is most important that you determine whether that animal has been vaccinated against rabies. If it is a wild animal, it is important that the animal be quarantined for at least two weeks. Call the animal warden in your area or contact your local animal shelter for information. You should call your veterinarian and ask his advice about a rabies booster for your dog.

Internal Parasites

The most common internal parasite of the dog is the **roundworm** (ascarid), which when vomited or passed through the rectum will often coil into a ring. These parasites are similar to strands of spaghetti and can be passed from the mother to the puppies. When you take your dog in for a checkup, take along a fresh stool sample. If it is posi-

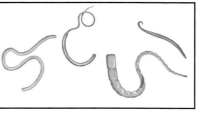

Common internal parasites (l-r): roundworm, whipworm, tapeworm and hookworm.

tive for roundworms, your vet will prescribe a safe worming agent, which will have to be repeated in two weeks to break the life cycle of the roundworms. Roundworms can not only affect the gastrointestinal tract but can pass into the lungs and cause damage there. You might suspect roundworms if your dog has an enlarged belly, poor weight gain, diarrhea or vomiting.

Hookworms are blood-suckers and can be transmitted either orally or by larval penetration of the skin. They attach themselves to the walls of the small intestine and feed on the blood of the dog. If left untreated, they can cause severe anemia and weight loss. Hookworms are much smaller than roundworms and are rarely detected by the owner. When treating your dog for hookworms, be sure to remove stools from your premises as the larvae can live in the soil; it may be necessary to treat your yard.

As adults, **whipworms** live in the caecum (a portion of the large intestine comparable to our appendix) and, like hookworms, are ingested from contaminated soil. If untreated, whipworms can cause diarrhea sometimes mixed with blood, anemia, weight loss and a prolapsed colon, a serious condition in which the rectal tissue of the lower colon everts and protrudes from the anus.

Tapeworm eggs are found in small, ricelike segments released from the anus of an infected dog. These segments are mobile and fall to the ground, where the eggs can be ingested by flea larvae in the environment. The tapeworm continues its development in the flea. When the flea is swallowed by the dog during his normal grooming, the tapeworm is released and completes its development in the dog.

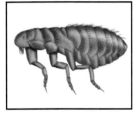

The flea is a die-hard pest.

Heartworm disease is caused by a filarial worm that is carried by mosquitoes. An early symptom is a cough, followed by the more serious symptoms of heart failure, because in the final stages the worm lives within the heart. Treatment for heartworm can be very hard on a dog and it is far better to give your dog a daily or monthly heartworm preventative. Some of the newer once-a-month heartworm preventatives also eliminate hookworms, roundworms and whipworms. Ask your vet what he or she recommends.

To avoid contamination or reinfestation of internal parasites, keep your premises clean and free of fecal matter by disposing of it in a proper manner. Make sure your dog has clean bedding and regular fecal checks approximately every six months. If you see him biting at his rear or trying to rub it on the floor, this could be an indication of worms.

Skin Problems

A dog with a healthy immune system is usually a dog with a healthy coat and skin. I wish I could say that *all* Shar-Pei have strong immune systems, but alas, some do not. Those lacking the necessary immunity to fight off some diseases suffer from immune-mediated skin diseases. While Shar-Pei have the reputation of having chronic skin problems, breeders have diligently tried, often with amazing success, to breed out some of the problems over the last decade. However, it is still not unusual for a Shar-Pei to experience a skin problem occasionally.

The skin of the Shar-Pei contains an overabundance of mucin, a gelatinous substance that is naturally present in all skin. In the Shar-Pei, it is mucin that contributes to the dog's charming wrinkles and nice padded muzzle. A Shar-Pei with an superabundance of mucin will sometimes have what appear to be little blisters usually found on the legs or head. These "blisters" are easily broken and will exude the gelatinous substance made up primarily of glycoprotein—mucin. These blisters are not harmful, though they can be unsightly, and do not mean that the dog will have other skin problems. The "blisters" do not cause problems themselves, but rupture of the bubbles, which may occur with excessive scratching or chewing, can spread the mucin on the skin surface and result in secondary bacterial skin disease.

One of the most common skin problems is an allergic reaction to external parasites such as fleas. Flea infestation can drive even the most experienced breeder to utter frustration and is especially problematic in warm, humid climates. At least in the northern areas of the country the fleas are killed off in the winter, but in the warmer climates it may seem that you can never rid your home of these pests, which can also be carriers of internal parasites. With the introduction of pyrethrins and permethrins (safe insecticides), killing these pests is at least nontoxic to our dogs.

You must inspect your dog on a regular basis during warm weather, especially if you notice him scratching or biting at himself around the tail region. Look for the

---

FIGHTING FLEAS

Remember, the fleas you see on your dog are only part of the problem—the smallest part! To rid your dog and home of fleas, you need to treat your dog *and* your home. Here's how:

• Identify where your pet(s) sleep. These are "hot spots."

• Clean your pets' bedding regularly by vacuuming and washing.

• Spray "hot spots" with a nontoxic, long-lasting flea larvicide.

• Treat outdoor "hot spots" with insecticide.

• Kill eggs on pets with a product containing insect growth regulators (IGRs).

• Kill fleas on pets per your veterinarian's recommendation.

black residue (feces) left by fleas. For every flea you find on your dog, probably a hundred more are lurking in your carpet, furniture or yard. Therefore, ridding your dog and your premises involves a three-pronged approach: You must first bathe your dog with a safe flea-killing shampoo, dip, or spray; then use a premises spray on your carpets and furniture; and thirdly, treat the outside area where your dog is exercised. I do not recommend flea collars for Chinese Shar-Pei because the insecticide in these collars can be absorbed into the skin and cause irritation or illness.

Bacterial dermatitis is a "catch-all" phrase that can refer to a range of skin infections usually caused by staphylococci which are commonly called "staph" infections. Certain conditions, however, must be present before a dog can have a staph infection, as staph will not invade normal, healthy skin. Systemic factors that may cause the skin to become abnormal and allow bacteria to invade are endocrine (hormonal) imbalances and immune deficiency disease. Hypothyroidism and female sex hormone imbalances are relatively common endocrine disorders. Skin problems in your puppy can indicate a puppy with lowered immunity; the resistant puppy with a stronger immune system will seldom have a skin problem. Stress can lower a dog's resistance to infection, especially in the case of the older dog.

Allergic inhalant disease can be a major cause of bacterial dermatitis. It is an allergic reaction to an inhaled substance in the dog's environment such as pollens, house dust and molds. It is a hereditary allergy and usually develops between one and three years of age, and in about 80 percent of the cases, it is

WHEN TO CALL THE VET

In any emergency situation, you should call your veterinarian immediately. You can make the difference in your dog's life by staying as calm as possible when you call and by giving the doctor or the assistant as much information as possible before you leave for the clinic. That way, the vet will be able to take immediate, specific action to remedy your dog's situation.

Emergencies include acute abdominal pain, suspected poisoning, snakebite, burns, frostbite, shock, dehydration, abnormal vomiting or bleeding, and deep wounds. You are the best judge of your dog's health, as you live with and observe him every day. Don't hesitate to call your veterinarian if you suspect trouble.

seasonal. The symptoms of allergies in dogs are very different from those of people. While we humans will sneeze, cough, have a runny nose, and so forth, the dog will have itchy skin, with the feet, face and ears being the most affected. While not curable, allergic inhalant disease is treatable. Antihistamines are safe and help to decrease itching in some dogs. Hypo-sensitization (allergy injections) requires a series of skin tests to determine the dog's specific allergies. A mild dose of cortisone is safe if given on an alternate-day basis and for a short period of time.

Hives may also result from inhalant allergies. One of my Shar-Pei could be counted on to develop hives every spring, and she was miserable until they sub-sided. Hives are raised red bumps that itch, and the dog will scratch unmercifully, causing them to ooze mucin and sometimes blood. Hives usually begin on the head but may spread to all parts of the body. Stress can also be a factor in developing hives.

Pyoderma is a bacterial infection of the skin and hair follicles. Mild forms may be treated with medicated shampoos containing peroxide, sulfur, tar or iodine and an antibiotic that should be continued for three or four weeks. Stubborn bacterial skin infections should be cultured for sensitivity to other antibi-otics that will be more effective. See your veteri-narian for a proper diag-nosis and treatment.

Demodectic mange is caused by mites that attack the skin; it can be a genetic condition.

Demodectic mange is one of the most common caus-es of skin problems in the Shar-Pei and is exacer-bated by a weakened immune system. It is caused by a mite that is present on the skin of all dogs, but it is the dog with a weaker immune system that allows the mange mite to multiply and attack the skin. Puberty is a stressful period for most dogs, and it is at this age, between six and twelve months, that the first symptoms of demodex are noticed. If you notice red, scaly spots that seem to be irritating to the dog, you must visit your veterinarian.

Two syndromes can occur: localized, which occurs primarily in dogs under one year of age, and generalized, which occurs in dogs over one year of age. Localized demodectic mange is usually self-limiting, and topical treatment with dips is not necessary. When the animal's immune system normalizes, the localized demodectic mange will resolve. Seldom does the localized form develop into the generalized form. Generalized demodectic mange is also known as "adult-onset" demodectic mange. It usually occurs in adults and indicates severe underlying systemic disease. It is more difficult to treat and is often complicated by secondary bacterial infections and self-trauma to the skin. The diagnosis of generalized demodecosis carries a guarded prognosis.

If this condition becomes chronic, it must be considered an immunodeficiency disease, which is hereditary, and the dog that develops it should not be bred. A dog with generalized demodecosis will soon develop an odor much like dirty, old sneakers, which frequent baths dispel only temporarily.

Another common cause of skin problems in Shar-Pei is **hypothyroidism,** which is caused by malfunctioning thyroid glands. These glands are part of the endocrine system and are located just in front of the larynx. In the more susceptible breeds (including the Chinese Shar-Pei), the symptoms usually begin between two and five years of age but can manifest earlier. These symptoms include lethargy, lack of endurance, thickening and darkening of the skin (called "elephant skin"), dry and brittle coats, loss of hair over the body in a symmetrical pattern, and skin that is prone to a variety of ills such as repeated pyodermas, seborrhea and bacterial infections. Fertility is often affected: Bitches will have irregular heat cycles, and males may have a lack of libido and become sterile. It is believed to be genetic, but fortunately, upon diagnosis, can be reversed with therapy.

Sarcoptic mange (Scabies) is another type of skin disease caused by a different mite than the one that causes demodecosis. Skin scrapings can also detect this mite, and dippings are the usual form of treatment. Scabies differs from demodectic mange in that it is highly contagious and can be transmitted to humans.

Interdigital dermatitis is a redness sometimes accompanied by swelling between the toes of a Shar-Pei and is most often caused by allergies—usually to grass, hypothyroidism or demodectic mange mites. Most puppies seem to outgrow this condition by one year of age, but others do not and will constantly chew at their feet. Soaking your dog's feet in a vinegar-water solution, applying athlete's foot sprays and powders, or using an Epsom salts solution have all been suggested as helpful.

Ringworm is a fungus (not a worm) infection on the surface of the skin. It appears as a round scaly area, red at first; then the hair within the circle falls out, leaving small bald spots in the coat. It is highly contagious among cats and dogs and can be passed on to humans. If positively diagnosed, all the animals in the household must be treated for at least six weeks, usually with a medication prescribed by your vet. Chronic cases may seem to clear up but can actually lay dormant until another outbreak. This is not a serious skin disease, but it can be unsightly because of the "holes" in the coat.

Use tweezers to remove ticks from your dog.

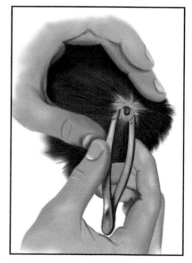

Ticks

This is another external parasite that, though it does not produce more than a short-lived skin reaction, can carry a myriad of other, more serious illnesses such as Rocky Mountain spotted fever, Lyme disease (discussed earlier in this chapter) and canine ehrlichiosis. The most common symptoms of this last disease are lack of appetite, lethargy, weight loss, vomiting, pale membranes in the mouth, lymph node enlargement and blood in the feces. Your veterinarian can prescribe treatment.

It is most important that you check your dog for ticks, especially in the spring and summer when they are most abundant. Ticks reside in grass, shrubs and trees and will take every opportunity to attach themselves to you or your dog to feed on blood. Some are so small as to go unnoticed, such as the deer tick which is a carrier of Lyme disease. If you find a tick attached to you or your dog, use tweezers to gently remove it, holding the tweezers as close to the skin as possible so as to remove all of the tick. Place it in a small container filled with alcohol. If you or your dog becomes ill, you may want to confirm that the tick was a carrier of one of the aforementioned diseases.

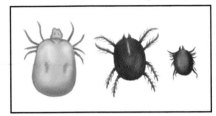

Three types of ticks (l-r): the wood tick, brown dog tick and deer tick.

FSF, Swollen Hock Syndrome and Systemic Amyloidosis

The following discussion will be very important to Shar-Pei owners. The terms FSF, swollen hock syndrome, and systemic amyloidosis describe a medical phenomenon that, although not unique to the Shar-Pei community, has been devastating to those owners whose dogs have suffered from one or all of these conditions. All the following information has been provided and approved by Linda Tintle, D.V.M., (Wurtsboro Veterinary Clinic, Wurtsboro, New York), a dedicated Shar-Pei owner who serves on the Health Through Education Committee of the CSPCA and has been collaborating with Dr. Ariel Rivas and Dr. Fred Quimby at Cornell University to explain the unusual and frustrating disorders affecting some Shar-Pei.

FSF refers to Familial Shar-Pei Fever, which is similar to Familial Mediterranean Fever (FMF), an inherited disorder characterized by recurrent episodes of fever accompanied by chest pain, abdominal pain or joint pain. The cause of FMF is unknown, but it is generally accepted to be a disorder of the regulation of the immune system.

FSF appears to be a similar disease. Shar-Pei are twenty-eight times more likely than dogs of other breeds to be presented to a veterinarian with acute fever of unknown origin. Pedigree analysis has provided evidence that FSF is undoubtedly an inherited disorder.

Joint swelling called "Swollen Hock Syndrome" (SHS) and associated joint pain and lameness may or may not accompany the fever. The swelling seems to be cellulitis or simple inflammation of the skin without infection. Other symptoms might include abdominal pain as demonstrated by a roached or arched back; reluctance to move or a stiff walk, sometimes accompanied by diarrhea and, occasionally, vomiting; and a firm, swollen and, less frequently, somewhat painful muzzle.

As is the case with Familial Mediterranean Fever, no tests are available to diagnose Familial Shar-Pei Fever or Swollen Hock Syndrome. A diagnosis can be difficult to ascertain. Routine tests will be unremarkable in most cases. Elevations in liver and kidney enzyme levels should be evaluated with amyloidosis in mind.

Treatment of the fever by owners depends upon the severity of the symptoms. Here I will digress from veterinary reports to relate my personal experiences with Shar-Pei suffering from fevers without the accompanying swollen hocks sometimes experienced. Several of my dogs, beginning ten years ago with one of my bitches, have had recurrent fevers. Her first episode occurred at eight weeks of age. I was alarmed when it first occurred, but she was treated with an antibiotic and returned to normal. As time has gone by, I have come to expect these periodic fevers that occur as often as every three months or as far apart as nine months. I now recognize the early symptoms such as not eating her evening meal, becoming very quiet and wanting to be alone. Then I watch for shivering, which is a certain signal that the fever is beginning. Even before this happens, I may take her temperature, but I do not begin any treatment unless the fever exceeds 102.5°F. The fever usually begins in the late afternoon or early evening, and by the time it has reached 103°F, it is evident that she is uncomfortable and is walking very stiffly. By this time the situation is serious enough that I either treat her myself or head for the emergency clinic. To get the fever down, I rely on one coated aspirin and an antibiotic provided by my veterinarian that I keep on hand. By bedtime, I can usually see that the fever has reversed its direction and is coming down. By the next morning, her temperature is back to normal (101°F), and she is apparently feeling better and ready to eat her breakfast. This routine has become a rather familiar one in our home, especially since we have added other Shar-Pei who from time to time have the same symptoms and respond in the same way to this treatment.

Mischevious puppies can get into unexpected trouble, so make sure you are prepared for an emergency before it happens.

Shar-Pei with FSF are at risk for premature death from amyloidosis. Amyloidosis is a broad term for a collection of diseases that result in the abnormal deposition of amyloid protein throughout the body. The damage or disease that results depends on what kind of body cell is most severely damaged or killed by these irregular deposits. Kidneys can't heal themselves by growing new kidney cells; if a kidney cell dies, it is gone for good and can't be replaced. This is why the amyloid protein usually causes kidney failure first.

Obviously, it would be very helpful if we had a screening test to identify carriers and affected animals, but we must be realistic. This disorder has been the focus of research for fifty years in people with FMF, and they have not yet developed a test. We hope that by using the Chinese Shar-Pei as a model for the human disease, it will allow more rapid progress and benefit both species. To that end, the Chinese Shar-Pei Club of America established a Charitable Trust in 1994 to help fund research to develop such a test.

Talk to your veterinarian about these related conditions and ways to recognize possible symptoms in your Shar-Pei.

Cancer in the Shar-Pei

Because of the weaker immune system of some Shar-Pei, they can be considered at risk for all types of cancer. The skin is the most common site for tumors in the Shar-Pei, though not all skin tumors are malignant. Most dermal or skin melanomas in the dog are benign. If found in the mouth of a dog, however, a melanoma is highly malignant and can spread to the lymph system or lungs if not caught early. Mast cell is a common skin tumor in Shar-Pei, and though it may or may not be malignant, it should be surgically removed. Breast cancer is very common, especially in the older, unspayed bitch. Fifty percent of breast tumors in dogs become malignant and may spread to other parts of the body, especially the lungs. Testicular cancer (cancer of the prostate) occurs most commonly in intact male dogs. Neutering greatly reduces the incidence of these malignancies.

To give a pill, open the mouth wide, then drop it in the back of the throat.

Eighteen years ago, the veterinary study of oncology did not even exist. Today, clinics are able to hire specialists in the field and obtain the vital equipment needed to treat various types of cancer in dogs. Treatments such as radiation, chemotherapy or immunotherapy (agents that stimulate the patient's own immune system to fight the cancer) can be expensive but are available. Some pet insurance programs will cover a portion of the costs. To locate a treatment center, ask your veterinarian, check with your nearest school of veterinary medicine or contact the local chapter of the Veterinary Medical Association.

Myositis is a disease that attacks a group of muscles. Masticatory myositis can progress or recurrent episodes can result in atrophy and fibrosis of the muscles that close the jaw; the end result is the inability to open the mouth. This is most likely an immune-mediated condition.

Symptoms include swelling of the temporalis muscles (in the temples between the ear and eye) and masseter muscles (muscles of the jaw), causing the dog to have "bugged" eyes; fever; enlarged lymph nodes; depression; and an inability to open the mouth—sometimes less than one-fourth of an inch—making it impossible to eat. Your vet may treat the condition with steroids.

Eye Care

Squeeze eye ointment into the lower lid.

In past years, eye problems in the Chinese Shar-Pei were much more common than they are today. With careful breeding of those animals with no eye problems, some of the hereditary problems such as entropion are becoming much less prevalent. However, it is still important to be aware of the conditions that can occur in your dog's eyes.

Watch for excess tearing or any matter exuding from your dog's eyes. This can occur during pollen season and is usually transitory, but it can be an early symptom of entropion, which is a weakness of the eye muscles that allows the eyelids to turn inward, causing the eyelashes to rub against the cornea. This eventually causes corneal scratching and if not corrected can cause corneal ulcers and even blindness.

To alleviate the abrasion of the cornea temporarily, an over-the-counter ointment used by contact lens wearers may be used in the dog's eyes. This simply sets up a barrier to help protect the eyes until you can see a veterinarian. If there is a minor infection present, your veterinarian may want to prescribe a triple antibiotic ointment. To administer ointment or drops, hold the dog firmly, pull the eyelid down, and drop the solution in behind the eyelid. This should be done quickly and firmly.

This may be all that is needed, but if entropion occurs during the puppy stage (up to eight months of age), the usual recommended treatment is eyetacking. The veterinarian will anesthetize the dog, evert the lids and tack them open with sutures. This allows the eye to heal and, hopefully, return to normal. The tissues of the eyelids are very tender, and you must watch for eye tacks that may pull out after a few days or sutures that are turning into the cornea. Veterinary ophthalmologists recommend using silk for sutures, but some veterinarians use stiff plastic material, which if trimmed too short can turn into the eye and rupture the cornea. This will cause blindness, and the eye may have to be removed. The sutures are removed after ten days to two weeks.

Fortunately eye problems in the Shar-Pei are less common than they used to be, but owners should be aware of possible conditions and their symptoms.

As the puppy's face develops, the need for eyetacking may not be necessary. If after repeated eyetackings, however, the eyelids continue to turn in, entropion surgery will be necessary. This is accomplished by the

77

veterinarian everting the eyelid, removing an eliptical section of skin with underlying muscle to correct alignment, and suturing the incision.

While rare, adult onset of entropion can happen. Stress and weight loss can be factors leading to adult entropion. A one-time eyetacking may correct the condition, but adult cases usually require entropion surgery.

The older dog may eventually develop **cataracts,** a partial or total opacity (cloudiness) of the lens within the eye. While this most commonly occurs in older dogs, cataracts can occur at any age as the result of trauma to the eye, and are sometimes even present at birth. Surgery can usually correct the condition.

Ears

While small and close to the head, Shar-Pei ears are extremely mobile, which allows for more air circulation than the ears of drop-eared dogs such as the Basset or Cocker Spaniel. Occasional cleaning to remove wax buildup should be routine. (See chapter 6, Grooming.)

If your dog scratches at his ear, shakes his head a lot, or tilts his head with his ear lowered, he probably has an ear infection. An infected ear will emit a distinct odor. See your veterinarian for treatment. If the problem is a chronic one, you should also have your vet check for ear mites (parasites that invade the ear and cause itching and inflammation) and/or a yeast infection. Shar-Pei who have problems with allergies will often have chronic ear problems, and if this occurs, your veterinarian may recommend an ear resection. This is a surgical procedure in which the veterinarian opens up the ear with a lateral incision so that air can more easily circulate.

Soft Tissue Problems

"Tight lip" is a condition that is apparently unique to the Chinese Shar-Pei. It occurs when the lower lip is especially thick and rolls up and over the lower incisor teeth. This can be a minor problem that causes the dog no problem, but in extreme cases it can push developing teeth back and prevent the dog from eating properly (when he chews, he bites his bottom lip). See your vet for surgical treatment.

Upper airway obstruction is known as brachycephalic airway obstruction syndrome and consists of stenotic nostrils, an elongated soft palate and often, everted laryngeal saccules. The dog with this condition is relatively heat-intolerant and susceptible to heat stress. The problem is not uncommon in brachy-cephalic dogs such as the Old English Bulldog, and the Shar-Pei too does not completely escape. Almost all Shar-Pei snore, some more than others, indicating a slightly **elongated soft palate.** With most, this is never a problem. However, if the soft palate (uvula) is too long, it can obstruct the airway and breathing becomes difficult. It is first noticed in the young dog who does not play as hard as his littermates, and gets easily overheated and stressed. According to Dr. David Saylor, a soft tissue specialist, the dog with an elongated soft palate is also prone to **stenotic nares,** or narrow nostrils that flow into also narrowed nasal passages. If the dog blows bubbles from his nose after he has been exercising, it is an indication of stenotic nares. In the normal breathing pattern the nostrils move back and forth as the dog breathes. With stenotic nares, the nostrils tend to close, cutting off normal air flow.

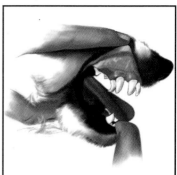

Check your dog's teeth frequently and brush them regularly.

Surgery is necessary to correct both stenotic nares and elongated soft palate, either by removing a portion of the nostril or shortening the palate. If these conditions aren't corrected, they can eventually lead to laryngeal problems, which are not as easily corrected.

Fortunately, most puppies who have only a slightly longer palate will "grow into" their palates and as adults have no breathing problems. For this reason, surgery is best postponed, if possible, until after six months of age.

Skeletal Problems

Hip Dysplasia is a malformation of the hip sockets that allows excessive movement in the joint, causing chronic inflammation and thus further breakdown and the deposit of calcium. After years, severe arthritis may result. The veterinary profession generally regards this as a genetic problem complicated by a variety of environmental influences. While many dogs with hip dysplasia do not exhibit symptoms until old age, others will often exhibit a crippling lameness early in life.

An accurate diagnosis may be made by reading a pelvic radiograph. The Orthopedic Foundation for Animals recommends diagnosing hip dysplasia when the dog is two years old, at which time a group of board-certified veterinary radiologists will evaluate your dog's

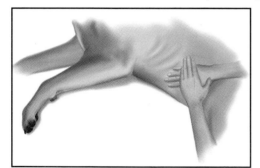

Applying abdominal thrusts can save a choking dog.

hips. If they determine that your dog is dysplastic, he should not be be bred, as this disease is considered hereditary.

The Chinese Shar-Pei has made great strides in the incidence of hip dysplasia. According to OFA statistics, the Shar-Pei has dropped from 21.4 percent to 9.2 percent dysplastic, or a reduced frequency of 50 percent to 60 percent. This is directly due to the fact that conscientious breeders are having their breeding stock evaluated for hip dysplasia and breeding only those dogs with good hips.

Patella luxation happens when the patella or kneecap in the rear leg slips out of place (sometimes called "slipping stifles"). This condition can also cause the dog to limp, and if lameness persists, surgery will be necessary to correct the problem. Though this is more often a problem in smaller breeds, Shar-Pei have been known to suffer from patella luxation.

Elbow dysplasia occurs when the dog exhibits lameness due to abnormal development of the elbow joint. To diagnose, an X ray is necessary. A surgical procedure can correct this problem, but affected animals should not be bred as it is thought to be hereditary. OFA will also evaluate your dog's X ray for elbow dysplasia.

Anal Glands

The anal glands are located on each side just below the dog's anus. You may notice that your dog will voluntarily empty his anal sacs after a bowel movement or if angered or distressed, and the odor is unmistakable. Routine evacuation is nature's way of cleansing these glands. However, if you notice your dog "scooting" his rear on the floor, it can mean one of two things: he may have worms, or he may have impacted anal glands caused by secretion buildup. In the latter case, these glands may need expressing. This is an unpleasant job I would rather leave to my veterinarian, but some owners do not find this task as objectionable as I do. Make sure the secretion buildup has not caused an abscess. If one of the glands is infected, the skin will be red and inflamed and you may see pus coming from the rectum. If you suspect an infection, this calls for veterinary intervention.

To complete this task, it is best to wear rubber gloves and gently probe the area with your thumb and forefinger until you locate the small, round gland. Gently express the contents of the gland into a soft cloth or tissue. This is sometimes a two-person job, one to hold the dog's head and talk to him gently and another to do "the dirty deed." If the glands become impacted or infected on a regular basis, your veterinarian may recommend that they be removed.

Reproductive Organs

Although the **testicles** in male puppies are present at birth, they do not descend into the scrotum until several weeks of age—some sooner, others later. Ask your vet to check for testicles in your new puppy if they are not visually evident when he gets his first vaccination. If they are not "down," don't worry yet. You probably have a late bloomer. Once the testicles have descended, it is possible for the puppy to "pull them up" because it takes some time for them to become firmly entrenched in the scrotum.

If, after six months, the testicle(s) are not down, consult with your veterinarian, and if they have not descended by one year, you should have him neutered. A great number of cancers occur in undescended testicles.

SPAYING AND NEUTERING

The term "neutering" generally refers to surgical sterilization of either sex. "Spaying" refers to neutering the bitch, and "castration" refers to neutering the male dog. Unless you plan to breed your bitch (and this is a very big decision), spaying the female dog is preferred for a number of reasons. First and foremost is to prevent pregnancy and subsequent unwanted litters. The recent increase in the number of Shar-Pei in animal shelters points out an emerging problem—unwanted Shar-Pei. Can you be sure to provide loving homes for any puppies your Shar-Pei may have? Do you really want to go through a heat cycle every six months? Unless you can accept all the responsibility involved in breeding your Shar-Pei, it is probably better to have her spayed.

The decision may be taken out of your hands if your female develops any one of several conditions that require she be spayed. These diseases include pyometra (severe uterine infection), uterine torsion (twisted uterus), uterine prolapse or tumors. Spaying is also recommended in the treatment of ovarian cysts. This surgery also helps in the control of some diseases such as diabetes or epilepsy and is good preventive medicine. If it is done before the first heat cycle, the incidence of breast tumors later in life decreases to less than .5 percent. Bear in mind that about 50 percent of breast tumors in female dogs are malignant. Finally, it is widely observed and documented that there is a higher incidence of immune-mediated diseases, such as systemic lupus erythematosus, and autoimmune hemolytic anemia, in intact female dogs.

Many veterinarians prefer to spay bitches prior to their first heat cycle. In the Shar-Pei, this usually means sometime between six and eight months of age. Early spaying of bitches apparently has no effect on the growth or health of the bitch and, as discussed, does reduce the incidence of breast tumors. Talk to your vet to decide the best time for your dog.

The surgery itself is relatively simple, and post-operative pain seems to be minimal, with most Shar-Pei up and around the day after. Aftercare is also minimal, and usually involves cleaning the incision for the first few days with hydrogen peroxide and keeping the dog from bothering the incision line.

Castration of the male dog is likewise valuable from a health standpoint. Castration helps in the prevention of testicular disease such as tumors, infection and trauma. It is also useful in eliminating

ADVANTAGES OF SPAY/NEUTER

The greatest advantage of spaying (for females) or neutering (for males) your dog is that you are guaranteed your dog will not produce puppies. There are too many puppies already available for too few homes. There are other advantages as well.

ADVANTAGES OF SPAYING

No messy heats.

No "suitors" howling at your windows or waiting in your yard.

Decreased incidences of pyometra (disease of the uterus) and breast cancer.

ADVANTAGES OF NEUTERING

Lessens male aggressive and territorial behaviors, but doesn't affect the dog's personality. Behaviors are often owner-induced, so neutering is not the only answer, but it is a good start.

Prevents the need to roam in search of bitches in season.

Decreased incidences of urogenital diseases.

or at least reducing some sexually related behaviors such as masking behavior, some forms of aggression, roaming, and so forth. The procedure involves a pre-scrotal incision through which both testicles are removed. Many veterinarians close the skin using sutures that require no post-operative follow-up visit;

they are simply absorbed by the body. Aftercare involves restricting activity for several days to prevent the scrotum from filling up with fluid. Most veterinarians recommend castration be done early in the dog's life, usually at eight to ten months of age when the dog is sexually mature, both for the prevention of disease and because of the fact that the young dog is a much better surgical risk.

Early spay/neuter, also known as "early-age neutering," has recently been endorsed by both the American Kennel Club and the American Veterinary Medical Association. The AKC recommends that breeders encourage puppy purchasers to have their pets spayed or neutered to prevent accidental breeding and to avoid breeding merely to produce puppies.

Emergency Treatment

Situations may occur that require emergency treatment. Discuss with your veterinarian what to do if an emergency arises. Does he or she have after-hours emergency care at his or her clinic? If not, where is the closest emergency clinic? You may not have time to get answers to these questions when an emergency arises, and it seems that emergencies invariably happen at night. Keep the number of the nearest emergency clinic near your telephone, and call ahead, if possible, to alert them to what the problem might be.

Make a temporary splint by wrapping the leg in firm casing, then bandaging it.

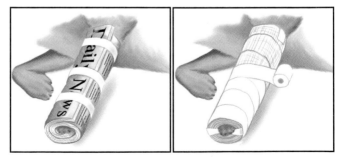

Always keep these emergency supplies on hand: a rectal thermometer, petroleum jelly, a soft muzzle, hydrogen peroxide or anitbacterial wash, an over-the-counter antihistamine, and a crate that you can quickly put in your car to transport an injured or sick dog. If you are alone and have no one to accompany you to an emergency clinic, you will need to keep your dog confined so that you can safely drive the car. Over-the-counter medications that may prove helpful in an emergency are aspirin, syrup of ipecac and antibiotic ointment.

ACCIDENTS

Your dog can be seriously injured in any number of accidents. It will always be better if there are two persons to assist in getting your dog to an emergency clinic when she is injured. (Someday, I foresee ambulance services for injured pets.) This is the time when a soft muzzle is helpful—either made of soft cloth or straps that have Velcro closures. If no muzzle is handy, you can use a strip of cloth, gauze or panty hose. Simply wrap the dog's muzzle, then make one tie under the chin, then around the neck and another more secure tie behind the head. If the dog is in a great deal of pain, she may bite without realizing you are trying to help. If she is bleeding, you must apply pressure at the point of bleeding or just above, at a point nearer the heart to try to stop the bleeding. If there are any evident broken bones, you can temporarily splint leg bones with rolls of newspaper. Wrap the dog in a blanket and go to the nearest emergency clinic.

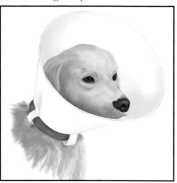

An Elizabethan collar keeps your dog from licking a fresh wound.

BLOAT

A very real emergency situation is bloat (gastric dilatation volvulus or GDV). This is a condition that is all too familiar to me, as I have lost five Shar-Pei to bloat. Bloat is the accumulation of gas bubbles in the stomach, causing the distention of the stomach. The first symptoms usually occur after the evening meal, but can occur after any meal. The dog will appear uncomfortable, will pace and salivate, attempt to drink water, then perhaps lick the floor or carpet. He may try to lie down, only to get up again and continue pacing. Gradually the stomach will begin to distend as if something is "blowing him up" like a balloon. He will try to vomit and if he can, this is a good sign. It means the stomach has not rotated on itself as yet.

With any of these symptoms, treatment must be sought immediately! If the condition persists, the stomach will turn, rotating on itself (called volvus) so that surgery becomes the only alternative if the animal recovers at all. Eventually the torsion, or twisting, cuts off the blood supply, blocking blood flow to the stomach and spleen; pressure builds on the heart, and the dog goes into shock. The pain is excruciating. Though theories exist, no one really knows what causes bloat. It is believed that large meals of dry food continually cause the stomach to expand then contract so that muscle tone is lost, or that exercise after a meal is a contributing factor. None of these caused my Shar-Pei to bloat, and my personal experience tells me stress can be an important contributing factor.

Bloat does not seem to follow a pattern or occur under the same circumstances; this is one life-threatening situation about which you cannot generalize. You must become aware of the symptoms. Feeding two or three smaller meals a day makes more sense than feeding one large one, and soaking your dog's food in an equal amount of water one-half hour before feeding makes sense. Warn your veterinarian that bloat is a problem in Shar-Pei and to monitor your dog carefully if he is recovering from anesthesia. Shar-Pei from the age of eleven weeks to fifteen years have bloated, so don't ever let anyone tell you that it cannot happen to a puppy!

There are apparently two types or degrees of bloat—one involves only the stomach, and the other involves both the stomach and small intestine. This latter type is the type that affected my Shar-Pei. My vet attempted to save each of these dogs, but there was no hope. (All five were related.) I was able to get each of them to the vet's clinic within fifteen to thirty minutes—even that was too late, so apparently this condition had been coming on for some time. The only symptoms we had noticed were that from time to time, each of these dogs would attempt to lick the floor or carpet, even chew threads from the carpet (much like dogs will try to eat grass); then they would vomit a thick, foamy, white matter that is apparently the same matter which fills the stomach during bloat. After they threw up this matter, they seemed fine.

I have yet two more Shar-Pei who from time to time exhibited the same symptoms as those who died from bloat. That is past tense! About a year ago, I began giving both these Shar-Pei digestive enzymes twice daily before feeding them. The symptoms of licking the floor and vomiting white froth have disappeared and to date have not recurred. Please understand that this is not a scientific study and by no means is proof that digestive enzymes help prevent bloat. I am merely passing this information on because I believe it has helped to eliminate some of the digestive upsets in my dogs and may prove helpful to others. Talk with your veterinarian about possible measures to prevent bloat.

ALLERGIC REACTION

Insect bites such as bee, wasp or hornet stings or spider bites can cause mild to severe allergic reactions in the dog. The very allergic dog may have welts, the head and face may swell, and the dog may have respiratory distress. It is important to treat the more severe symptoms immediately. The usual mode of treatment is with antihistamines, steroids or epinephrine injection. For the minor sting or bite that is not accompanied by unusual reactions, make a paste of either meat tenderizer or baking soda, and watch the dog for several hours after he is stung.

CARDIAC ARREST

If your dog loses consciousness and you suspect **cardiac arrest**, place your thumb under one front leg and your four fingers in the other armpit areas to determine whether your dog's heart is still beating. This places the chest between your fingers. Reach up to feel for a heartbeat. If you cannot feel a heartbeat, put your ear on the dog's chest to listen for a heartbeat, then check for a pulse either in the side of the neck or inside the hind leg where the leg meets the body. A normal pulse rate is 80 to 140 beats per minute. Cardiopulmonary resuscitation (CPR) can be performed on a dog by first examining the dog's mouth to make sure the mouth and airway are clear. Then close the mouth and, holding it shut, blow three short breaths into the nose (watch to see the chest rise). Then, with the dog on his side, press down with two hands on the chest to stimulate the heart and force air in and out of the lungs. Chest compression should be rapid, and you should stop about every thirty seconds to see whether the heartbeat has resumed. Get the dog to an emergency clinic, giving the described CPR all the way, unless the dog begins breathing on his own.

DIARRHEA AND DEHYDRATION

While diarrhea in and of itself is not an emergency, it can be a symptom of another problem, and if not diagnosed and treated can cause dehydration. This can become an emergency and is particularly serious in young puppies. You can check to see whether a dog is seriously dehydrated by pulling up the skin on the back. If the skin feels plump and quickly returns to its normal position, the dog is probably not seriously dehydrated. However, if the skin feels pliable and remains "pulled up," then that is an indication that the dog/puppy is becoming dehydrated. Dry or "tacky" gums may also indicate dehydration. The dog probably is too sick to be expected to drink enough water to correct the condition. Take her to a veterinarian who, if he or she confirms dehydration, will inject fluids that are slowly absorbed into her body. This is only a temporary measure. Your vet must determine what is causing the diarrhea and resulting dehydration. Some of the causes of diarrhea may include parasites; bacterial or virile infections; spoiled or toxic food;

indigestible material such as hair, bones, sticks and so on; or stress.

After you have determined the cause of a bout of diarrhea and the condition has been treated, it is helpful to feed a bland diet for the first twenty-four hours to which you have added yogurt to restore the helpful flora to the intestinal tract.

HIGH FEVER

A high **fever** can be an emergency situation. There are many reasons for a fever, the most common being the onset of a bacterial or viral infection and, as we have discussed, FSF. Fever is not a disease but a signal by the body that something is wrong. You need to know how wrong! Always keep a rectal thermometer nearby and before using, rub petroleum jelly on the end of the thermometer. If the dog is very sick and lying down, gently rub her head and soothe her while inserting the thermometer into the rectum about two inches. Continue to talk to your dog, leaving the thermometer in the rectum for approximately one and a half to two minutes. If the dog is ambulatory, I like to hold the dog between my legs, lift her tail and insert the thermometer. I can still rub her head and soothe her this way.

How much fever is too much? A normal range for a dog's temperature is between 100.5°F to 101.5°F, with a .5°F leeway in either direction. If I suspect a fever, I take my dog's temperature, and if it is nearing 102°F, I become suspicious because I know that it should be closer to 101°F. I will be taking that dog's temperature again within an hour, and if it passes 102°F, the dog will get a coated aspirin (uncoated aspirin sometimes upsets the stomach). If it rises to 104°F, the vet gets a call; past 105°F, worry sets in; and past 106°F, it's panic time—get the dog to an emergency clinic. I know that high fevers can cause convulsions, hyperthermia and death. In addition to the aspirin, I use cold cloths on the head, belly and legs and have even put a dog in the bathtub to bring a fever down. In the case of a high fever, however, get your dog to a vet where the proper medication can be given to reduce the fever and a diagnosis can be made.

POISON

If your dog has been poisoned accidentally, you must try to find the source of poison so that when you call your veterinarian or poison control center they can accurately tell whether you should or should not induce vomiting. Most accidental poisonings are caused by household cleaning agents, fertilizers, poison put out for rodents, or antifreeze, which is apparently sweet and tasty to dogs, but also very deadly. Another common cause of poisonings is the ingestion of human drugs. Always keep your medications secured where your dog can't get to them.

Some of the many household substances harmful to your dog.

If your veterinarian instructs you to induce vomiting, you can administer ipecac, a syrup that can be purchased at your pharmacy and should be kept in your emergency kit. Take some of the vomitus with you to

the veterinarian so that he can determine the type of poison ingested by your dog.

Symptoms of poisoning vary with the type of poison ingested but can include vomiting or attempting to vomit, salivating, disorientation, loss of muscle control and convulsions.

The National Animal Poison Control Center has two emergency phone numbers for information: The first requires a credit card number (800)548-2423 and (900)680-0000 (charged to your phone at $20.00 for the first five minutes, then $2.95 for each additional minute).

HEATSTROKE

Unlike humans, dogs cannot sweat and can more easily become overheated. They pant to cool themselves and when panting is no longer adequate, their temperature begins to rise and can quickly reach dangerous limits. Never leave a dog in a closed car on a warm day or out in the sun too long even if they seem to like lying in the sun (and many Shar-Pei do). Shar-Pei are perhaps more heat-intolerant than other breeds due to the previously described brachycephalic airway obstruction syndrome, which interferes with normal heat exchange via the respiratory tract. Black Shar-Pei are much more susceptible to heat than the lighter-colored dogs because their dark color absorbs heat rays rather than reflecting them. Lighter-colored Shar-Pei such as the creams and dilutes are also very susceptible to sunburn. The overheated dog must be cooled immediately. If a hose is available, wet the dog with cool (not cold) water starting with the head or put the dog in a tub and run cool water over the dog until the temperature has dropped to 103°F or 102°F. Once the temperature is down, take the dog to a veterinarian for further treatment.

SHOCK

Shock is the result of severe illness, injury or internal bleeding, and the symptoms are weak pulse, shallow breathing, pale gums and dilated pupils. The body temperature drops and the circulatory system begins to shut down. Prompt veterinary care is imperative as this is a life-threatening condition. The dog must be kept warm at an even temperature, kept as quiet as possible and taken to an emergency clinic.

Run your hands regularly over your dog to feel for any injuries.

WILD ANIMAL ATTACKS

Wild animal attacks are not unusual, even in city or suburban living. Dogs are very inquisitive, and Shar-Pei are natural hunters who will most likely attack the wild animal first. Wild animals such as the skunk, the opossum or the raccoon have little chance of escaping from a Shar-Pei, but can inflict nasty bites. They can also be carriers of rabies. Do not neglect your dog's immunizations against this dreaded disease.

If a skunk sprays your dog, it can be very painful to his eyes, the area that seems to be just where the skunk takes aim. Wash your dog's eyes with warm water, and apply a few drops of vegetable or olive oil to them. If you have any ophthalmic ointment on hand (which many Shar-Pei owners do), that will also suffice to ease the pain to his eyes. The usual treatment for the overpowering skunk odor is a bath in tomato or lemon juice, which can be followed by soap and water.

When planning an outing in the country with your dog, take a few precautionary measures and a small first-aid kit—if not for you, for your dog. Include a small cloth muzzle, small knife, eye ointment, pliers, an antiseptic such as peroxide, meat tenderizer(for insect stings) and, should you anticipate meeting a porcupine, a small bottle of vinegar. If you are going into a part of the country where you know there are poisonous snakes, take along a snakebite kit.

Use a scarf or old hose to make a temporary muzzle, as shown.

If your Shar-Pei accompanies you on a trip to the country where he might encounter a porcupine, it is helpful to know what to do if your dog once again decides he is a mighty hunter. With the porcupine, I think your dog will lose the fight. If this happens, take your Shar-Pei to a veterinarian right away because **porcupine quills** will invade the tissues more and more as the dog moves around. If you are far away from a vet, you will have to remove the quills yourself as soon as possible. This should be done gradually and will be very painful for your dog and may necessitate using a muzzle. If one is not available, use a torn strip of fabric to tie his muzzle, twist it under the chin then behind the head and tie again. Beginning in the chest area, cut off the tips of the quills at an angle in order to release pressure, making them easier to remove (vinegar may also be used to soften the quills). Use an instrument such as pliers (if none are available, your fingers will have to do) to slowly twist out each quill—do not jerk them out. As they are removed, clean the wound with an antibacterial agent such as peroxide.

Snakebite is always a danger when hiking with your dog in the woods. Try to determine in one of two ways whether the snake is poisonous or nonpoisonous. Either kill the snake and examine its mouth (if the snake has two fangs that can be folded against the roof of the mouth, then it is poisonous), or if the snake cannot be found, examine your dog's wound (if the snakebite consists of two puncture wounds as opposed to a row of teeth marks, then it was made by a poisonous snake). Some poisonous snakes are more deadly than others, but if you determine that the snake is poisonous, do not delay getting your dog to a veterinarian. If the bite is on the leg, a tourniquet applied between the wound and the body will help delay the poison moving to other parts of the body, but most snakebites on the dog are in the head region and this is even more dangerous. Trying to cut into the puncture wounds will help little and may waste valuable time. Try to keep your dog calm and find a veterinarian immediately.

Euthanasia

The decision to euthanize your dog is never an easy one, but a pet owner needs to prepare for the eventuality of it since, in my experience, only about one of every ten animals will die outside of the veterinarian's office. The actual clinical procedure of euthanasia is simple, painless and peaceful. The solution administered is a powerful barbiturate anesthetic agent which is given intravenously as an overdose.

Making arrangements beforehand while the owner is more rational and clear-headed is very helpful. The veterinarian needs to know about the owner's decisions concerning the disposal of the body. Does the owner or other family members wish to be present during the euthanasia? As the time approaches, the veterinarian should be called and an appointment made. This assures that the doctor will not be rushed and will allow the family time to be with the pet before and after the procedure. Prior to leaving for the vet's office, the dog should be walked and allowed an opportunity to relieve himself.

The decision of when to euthanize a pet should be thoughtfully considered. Bear in mind that most disease processes have a long course which results in the gradual decline of the dog's health. I look at the quality of life of the dog in terms of good days and bad days. As long as the good days outnumber the bad days, the dog's quality of life is acceptable. Again, the owner must decide for him- or herself what constitutes an acceptable quality of life for his or her dog. *Do not force your veterinarian to make the euthanasia decision for you.* His or her job is to provide the information necessary to enable *you* to make your decision.

Often, I feel owners think they are betraying the trust of their pet when euthanasia is considered. Quite the opposite! I believe our dogs trust us to decide for them when life has become too much of a burden to continue. While they cannot directly relate this to us, the behavioral changes in the geriatric animal unmistakably tell us when euthanasia becomes an option. Death is a part of life and cannot be avoided, but the suffering and debilitation of old age or incurable disease are not natural; the infirm animal in the wild is the first to be eliminated. Life can end with dignity and compassion by living up to that trust in a final loving act of sacrifice on our part. Allow yourself to remember the good times spent with your best friend.

Author's Note: My thanks once again to Jeff Vidt, D.V.M., for allowing me to quote him in the discussion on euthanasia.

Your Happy, Healthy Pet

Your Dog's Name _____

Name on Your Dog's Pedigree (if your dog has one) _____
_____

Where Your Dog Came From _____
_____

Your Dog's Birthday _____

Your Dog's Veterinarian

    Name   _____

    Address   _____

    Phone Number_____

    Emergency Number_____

Your Dog's Health

    Vaccines

    type _____ date given _____

    type _____ date given _____

    type _____ date given _____

    type _____ date given _____

    Heartworm

    date tested _____ type used_____ start date _____

Your Dog's License Number_____

Groomer's Name and Number _____

Dogsitter/Walker's Name and Number_____

Awards Your Dog Has Won

    Award _____ date earned _____

    Award _____ date earned _____

part three

Enjoying

your

Dog

chapter 8

Basic
Training

by Ian Dunbar, Ph.D., MRCVS

Training is the jewel in the crown—the most important aspect of doggy husbandry. There is no more important variable influencing dog behavior and temperament than the dog's education: A well-trained, well-behaved and good-natured puppydog is always a joy to live with, but an untrained and uncivilized dog can be a perpetual nightmare. Moreover, deny the dog an education and it will not have the opportunity to fulfill its own canine potential; neither will it have the ability to communicate effectively with its human companions.

Luckily, modern psychological training methods are easy, efficient and effective and, above all, considerably dog-friendly and user-friendly. Doggy education is as simple as it is enjoyable. But before

98

you can have a good time play-training with your new dog, you have to learn what to do and how to do it. There is no bigger variable influencing the success of dog training than the *owner's* experience and expertise. *Before you embark on the dog's education, you must first educate yourself.*

Basic Training for Owners

Ideally, basic owner training should begin well *before* you select your dog. Find out all you can about your chosen breed first, then master rudimentary training and handling skills. If you already have your puppy/dog, owner training is a dire emergency—the clock is running! Especially for puppies, the first few weeks at home are the most important and influential days in the dog's life. Indeed, the cause of most adolescent and adult problems may be traced back to the initial days the pup explores his new home. This is the time to establish the *status quo*—to teach the puppy/dog how you would like him to behave and so prevent otherwise quite predictable problems.

In addition to consulting breeders and breed books such as this one (which understandably have a positive breed bias), seek out as many pet owners with your breed you can find. Good points are obvious. What you want to find out are the breed-specific *problems,* so you can nip them in the bud. In particular, you should talk to owners with *adolescent* dogs and make a list of all anticipated problems. Most important, *test drive* at least half a dozen adolescent and adult dogs of your breed yourself. An eight-week-old puppy is deceptively easy to handle, but she will acquire adult size, speed and strength in just four months, so you should learn now what to prepare for.

Puppy and pet dog training classes offer a convenient venue to locate pet owners and observe dogs in action. For a list of suitable trainers in your area, contact the Association of Pet Dog Trainers (see Chapter 13). You may also begin your basic owner training by observing other owners in class. Watch as many classes and test drive as many dogs as possible. Select an upbeat, dog-friendly, people-friendly, fun-and-games, puppydog pet training class to learn the ropes. Also, watch training videos and read training books (see Chapter 12). You must find out what to do and how to do it *before* you have to do it.

Principles of Training

Most people think training comprises teaching the dog to do things such as sit, speak and roll over, but even a four-week-old pup knows how to do these things already. Instead, the first step in training involves teaching the dog human words for each dog behavior and activity and for each aspect of the dog's environment. That way you, the owner, can more easily participate in the dog's domestic education by directing him to perform specific actions appropriately, that is, at the right time, in the right place, and so on. Training opens communication channels, enabling an educated dog to at least understand the owner's requests.

In addition to teaching a dog *what* we want her to do, it is also necessary to teach her *why* she should do what we ask. Indeed, 95 percent of training revolves around motivating the dog *to want to do* what we want. Dogs often understand what their owners want; they just don't see the point of doing it—especially when the owner's repetitively boring and seemingly senseless instructions are totally at odds with much more pressing and exciting doggy distractions. It is not so much the dog who is being stubborn or dominant; rather, it is the owner who has failed to acknowledge the dog's needs and feelings and to approach training from the dog's point of view.

The Meaning of Instructions

The secret to successful training is learning how to use training lures to predict or prompt specific behaviors—to coax the dog to do what you want *when* you want. Any highly valued object (such as a treat or toy) may be used as a lure, which the dog will follow with his eyes and nose. Moving the lure in specific ways entices the dog to move his nose, head and entire body in specific ways. In fact, by learning the art of manipulating various lures, it is possible to teach the dog to assume virtually any body position and perform any action. Once you have control over the expression of the dog's behaviors and can elicit any body position or behavior at will, you can easily teach the dog to perform on request.

Tell your dog what you want him to do, use a lure to entice him to respond correctly, then profusely praise

Teach your dog words for each activity he needs to know, like down.

and maybe reward him once he performs the desired action. For example, verbally request "Fido, sit!" while you move a squeaky toy upwards and backwards over the dog's muzzle (lure-movement and hand signal), smile knowingly as he looks up (to follow the lure) and sits down (as a result of canine anatomical engineering), then praise him to distraction ("Gooood Fido!"). Squeak the toy, offer a training treat and give your dog and yourself a pat on the back.

Being able to elicit desired responses over and over enables the owner to reward the dog over and over. Consequently, the dog begins to think training is fun. For example, the more the dog is rewarded for sitting, the more she enjoys sitting. Eventually the dog comes to realize that, whereas most sitting is appreciated, sitting immediately upon request usually prompts especially enthusiastic praise and a slew of high-level rewards. The dog begins to sit on cue much of the time, showing that she is starting to grasp the meaning of the owner's verbal request and hand signal.

Why Comply?

Most dogs enjoy initial lure/reward training and are only too happy to comply with their owners' wishes. Unfortunately, repetitive drilling without appreciative feedback tends to diminish the dog's enthusiasm until he eventually fails to see the point of complying anymore. Moreover, as the dog approaches adolescence he becomes more easily distracted as he develops other interests. Lengthy sessions with repetitive exercises tend to bore and demotivate both parties. If it's not fun, the owner doesn't do it and neither does the dog.

Integrate training into your dog's life: The greater number of training sessions each day and the *shorter* they are, the more willingly compliant your dog will become. Make sure to have a short (just a few seconds) training interlude before every enjoyable canine activity. For example, ask your dog to sit to greet people, to sit before you throw his Frisbee, and to sit for his supper. Really, sitting is no different from a canine "please." Also, include numerous short training interludes during every enjoyable canine pastime, for example, when playing with the dog or when he is running in the park. In this fashion, doggy distractions may be effectively converted into rewards for training. Just as all games have rules, fun becomes training . . . and training becomes fun.

Eventually, rewards actually become unnecessary to continue motivating your dog. If trained with consideration and kindness, performing the desired behaviors will become self-rewarding and, in a sense, your dog will motivate himself. Just as it is not necessary to reward a human companion during an enjoyable walk in the park, or following a game of tennis, it is hardly necessary to reward our best friend—the dog—for walking by our side or while playing fetch. Human company during enjoyable activities is reward enough for most dogs.

Even though your dog has become self-motivating, it's still good to praise and pet him a lot and offer rewards once in a while, especially for a good job well done. And if for no other reason, praising and rewarding others is good for the human heart.

To train your dog, you need gentle hands, a loving heart and a good attitude.

Punishment

Without a doubt, lure/reward training is by far the best way to teach: Entice your dog to do what you want and then reward him for doing so. Unfortunately, a human shortcoming is to take the good for granted and to moan and groan at the bad. Specifically, the dog's many good behaviors are ignored while the owner focuses on punishing the dog for making mistakes. In extreme cases, instruction is *limited* to punishing mistakes made by a trainee dog, child, employee or husband, even though it has been proven punishment training is notoriously inefficient and ineffective and is decidedly unfriendly and combative. It teaches the dog that training is a drag, almost as quickly as it teaches the dog to dislike his trainer. Why treat our best friends like our worst enemies?

Punishment training is also much more laborious and time consuming. Whereas it takes only a finite amount of time to teach a dog what to chew, for example, it takes much, much longer to punish the dog for each and every mistake. Remember, *there is only one right way!* So why not teach that right way from the outset?!

To make matters worse, punishment training causes severe lapses in the dog's reliability. Since it is obviously impossible to punish the dog each and every time she misbehaves, the dog quickly learns to distinguish between those times when she must comply (so as to avoid impending punishment) and those times when she need not comply, because punishment is impossible. Such times include when the dog is off leash and only six feet away, when the owner is otherwise engaged (talking to a friend, watching television, taking a shower, tending to the baby or chatting on the telephone), or when the dog is left at home alone.

Instances of misbehavior will be numerous when the owner is away, because even when the dog complied in the owner's looming presence, he did so unwillingly. The dog was forced to act against his will, rather than moulding his will to want to please. Hence, when the owner is absent, not only does the dog know he need not comply, he simply does not want to. Again, the trainee is not a stubborn vindictive beast, but rather the trainer has failed to teach.

Punishment training invariably creates unpredictable Jekyll and Hyde behavior.

Trainer's Tools

Many training books extol the virtues of a vast array of training paraphernalia and electronic and metallic gizmos, most of which are designed for canine restraint, correction and punishment, rather than for actual facilitation of doggy education. In reality, most effective training tools are not found in stores; they come from within ourselves. In addition to a willing dog, all you really need is a functional human brain, gentle hands, a loving heart and a good attitude.

In terms of equipment, all dogs do require a quality buckle collar to sport dog tags and to attach the leash (for safety and to comply with local leash laws). Hollow chewtoys (like Kongs or sterilized longbones) and a dog bed or collapsible crate are a must for housetraining. Three additional tools are required:

1. specific lures (training treats and toys) to predict and prompt specific desired behaviors;

2. rewards (praise, affection, training treats and toys) to reinforce for the dog what a lot of fun it all is; and

3. knowledge—how to convert the dog's favorite activities and games (potential distractions to training) into "life-rewards," which may be employed to facilitate training.

The most powerful of these is *knowledge*. Education is the key! Watch training classes, participate in training classes, watch videos, read books, enjoy playtraining with your dog, and then your dog will say "Please," and your dog will say "Thank you!"

Housetraining

If dogs were left to their own devices, certainly they would chew, dig and bark for entertainment and then no doubt highlight a few areas of their living space with sprinkles of urine, in much the same way we decorate by hanging pictures. Consequently, when we ask a dog to live with us, we must teach him *where* he may dig and perform his toilet duties, *what* he may chew and *when* he may bark. After all, when left at home alone for many hours, we cannot expect the dog to amuse himself by completing crosswords or watching the soaps on TV!

Also, it would be decidedly unfair to keep the house rules a secret from the dog, and then get angry and punish the poor critter for inevitably transgressing rules he did not even know existed. Remember, without adequate education and guidance, the dog will be forced to establish his own rules—doggy rules—that most probably will be at odds with the owner's view of domestic living.

Since most problems develop during the first few days the dog is at home, prospective dog owners must be certain they are quite clear about the principles of housetraining *before* they get a dog. Early misbehaviors quickly become established as the status quo—

becoming firmly entrenched as hard-to-break bad habits, which set the precedent for years to come. Make sure to teach your dog good habits right from the start. Good habits are just as hard to break as bad ones!

Ideally, when a new dog comes home, try to arrange for someone to be present for as much as possible during the first few days (for adult dogs) or weeks for puppies. With only a little forethought, it is surprisingly easy to find a puppy sitter, such as a retired person, who would be willing to eat from your refrigerator and watch your television while keeping an eye on the newcomer to encourage the dog to play with chewtoys and to ensure he goes outside on a regular basis.

POTTY TRAINING

To teach the dog where to relieve himself:

1. never let him make a single mistake;

2. let him know where you want him to go; and

3. handsomely reward him for doing so:
   "GOOOOOOOD DOG!!!" liver treat, liver treat, liver treat!

PREVENTING MISTAKES

A single mistake is a training disaster, since it heralds many more in future weeks. And each time the dog soils the house, this further reinforces the dog's unfortunate preference for an indoor, carpeted toilet. *Do not let an unhousetrained dog have full run of the house if you are away from home or cannot pay full attention.* Instead, confine the dog to an area where elimination is appropriate, such as an outdoor run or, better still, a small, comfortable indoor kennel with access to an outdoor run. When confined in this manner, most dogs will naturally housetrain themselves.

If that's not possible, confine the dog to an area, such as a utility room, kitchen, basement or garage, where elimination may not be desired in the long run but as an interim measure it is certainly preferable to doing it all around the house. Use newspaper to cover the floor of the dog's day room. The newspaper may be used to soak up the urine and to wrap up and dispose of the feces. Once your dog develops a preferred spot for eliminating, it is only necessary to cover that part of the floor with newspaper. The smaller papered area may then be moved (only a little each day) towards the door to the outside. Thus the dog will develop the tendency to go to the door when he needs to relieve himself.

Never confine an unhousetrained dog to a crate for long periods. Doing so would force the dog to soil the crate and ruin its usefulness as an aid for housetraining (see the following discussion).

The first few weeks at home are the most important and influential in your dog's life.

TEACHING WHERE

In order to teach your dog where you would like her to do her business, you have to be there to direct the proceedings—an obvious, yet often neglected, fact of life. In order to be there to teach the dog *where* to go, you need to know *when* she needs to go. Indeed, the success of housetraining depends on the owner's ability to predict these times. Certainly, a regular feeding schedule will facilitate prediction somewhat, but there is nothing like "loading the deck" and influencing the timing of the outcome yourself!

Whenever you are at home, make sure the dog is under constant supervision and/or confined to a small area. If already well trained, simply instruct the dog to lie down in his bed or basket. Alternatively, confine the dog to a crate (doggy den) or tie-down (a short, 18-inch lead that can be clipped to an eye hook in the baseboard). Short-term close confinement strongly inhibits urination and defecation, since the dog does not want to soil his sleeping area. Thus, when you release the puppydog each hour, he will definitely need to urinate immediately and defecate every third or fourth hour. Keep the dog confined to his doggy den and take him to his intended toilet area each hour, every hour, and on the hour.

When taking your dog outside, instruct him to sit quietly before opening the door—he will soon learn to sit by the door when he needs to go out!

TEACHING WHY

Being able to predict when the dog needs to go enables the owner to be on the spot to praise and reward the dog. Each hour, hurry the dog to the intended toilet area in the yard, issue the appropriate instruction ("Go pee!" or "Go poop!"), then give the dog three to four minutes to produce. Praise and offer a couple of training treats when successful. The treats are important because many people fail to praise their dogs with feeling . . . and housetraining is hardly the time for understatement. So either loosen up and enthusiastically praise that dog: "Wuzzzer-wuzzer-wuzzer, hoooser good wuffer den? Hoooo went pee for Daddy?" Or say "Good dog!" as best you can and offer the treats for effect.

Following elimination is an ideal time for a spot of playtraining in the yard or house. Also, an empty dog may be allowed greater freedom around the house for the next half hour or so, just as long as you keep an eye out to make sure he does not get into other kinds of mischief. If you are preoccupied and cannot pay full attention, confine the dog to his doggy den once more to enjoy a peaceful snooze or to play with his many chewtoys.

If your dog does not eliminate within the allotted time outside—no biggie! Back to his doggy den, and then try again after another hour.

As I own large dogs, I always feel more relaxed walking an empty dog, knowing that I will not need to finish our stroll weighted down with bags of feces! Beware of falling into the trap of walking the dog to get it to eliminate. The good ol' dog walk is such an enormous highlight in the dog's life that it represents the single biggest potential reward in domestic dogdom. However, when in a hurry, or during inclement weather, many owners abruptly terminate the walk the moment the dog has done its business. This, in effect, severely punishes the dog for doing the right thing, in the right place at the right time. Consequently, many dogs become strongly inhibited from eliminating outdoors because they know it will signal an abrupt end to an otherwise thoroughly enjoyable walk.

Instead, instruct the dog to relieve himself in the yard prior to going for a walk. If you follow the above instructions, most dogs soon learn to eliminate on cue. As soon as the dog eliminates, praise (and offer a treat or two)—"Good dog! Let's go walkies!" Use the walk as a reward for eliminating in the yard. If the dog does not go, put him back in his doggy den and think about a walk later on. You will find with a "No feces–no walk" policy, your dog will become one of the fastest defecators in the business.

If you do not have a back yard, instruct the dog to eliminate right outside your front door prior to the walk. Not only will this facilitate clean up and disposal of the feces in your own trash can but, also, the walk may again be used as a colossal reward.

CHEWING AND BARKING

Short-term close confinement also teaches the dog that occasional quiet moments are a reality of domestic living. Your puppydog is extremely impressionable during his first few weeks at home. Regular confinement at this time soon exerts a calming influence over the dog's personality. Remember, once the dog is housetrained and calmer, there will be a whole lifetime ahead for the dog to enjoy full run of the house and garden. On the other hand, by letting the newcomer have unrestricted access to the entire household and allowing him to run willy-nilly, he will most certainly develop a bunch of behavior problems in short order, no doubt necessitating confinement later in life. It would not be fair to remedially restrain and confine a dog you have trained, through neglect, to run free.

When confining the dog, make sure he always has an impressive array of suitable chewtoys. Kongs and sterilized longbones (both readily available from pet stores) make the best chewtoys, since they are hollow and may be stuffed with treats to heighten the dog's interest. For example, by stuffing the little hole at the top of a Kong with a small piece of freeze-dried liver, the dog will not want to leave it alone.

Remember, treats do not have to be junk food and they certainly should not represent extra calories. Rather, treats should be part of each dog's regular daily diet:

Make sure your puppy has suitable chewtoys.

Some food may be served in the dog's bowl for breakfast and dinner, some food may be used as training treats, and some food may be used for stuffing chewtoys. I regularly stuff my dogs' many Kongs with different shaped biscuits and kibble. The kibble seems to fall out fairly easily, as do the oval-shaped biscuits, thus rewarding the dog instantaneously for checking out the chewtoys. The bone-shaped biscuits fall out after a while, rewarding the dog for worrying at the chewtoy. But the triangular biscuits never come out. They remain inside the Kong as lures, maintaining the dog's fascination with its chewtoy. To further focus the dog's interest, I always make sure to flavor the triangular biscuits by rubbing them with a little cheese or freeze-dried liver.

If stuffed chewtoys are reserved especially for times the dog is confined, the puppy-dog will soon learn to enjoy quiet moments in her doggy den and she will quickly develop a chewtoy habit—a good habit! This is a simple *passive training* process; all the owner has to do is set up the situation and the dog all but trains herself—easy and effective. Even when the dog is given run of the house, her first inclination will be to indulge her rewarding chewtoy habit rather than destroying less-attractive household articles, such as curtains, carpets, chairs and compact disks. Similarly, a chewtoy chewer will be less inclined to scratch and chew herself excessively. Also, if the dog busies herself as a recreational chewer, she will be less inclined to develop into a recreational barker or digger when left at home alone.

Stuff a number of chewtoys whenever the dog is left confined and remove the extra-special-tasting treats when you return. Your dog will now amuse himself with his chewtoys before falling asleep and then resume playing with his chewtoys when he expects you to return. Since most owner-absent misbehavior happens right after you leave and right before your expected return, your puppydog will now be conveniently preoccupied with his chewtoys at these times.

Come and Sit

Most puppies will happily approach virtually anyone, whether called or not; that is, until they collide with

To teach come, call your dog, open your arms as a welcoming signal, wave a toy or a treat and praise for every step in your direction.

adolescence and develop other more important doggy interests, such as sniffing a multiplicity of exquisite odors on the grass. Your mission, Mr. and/or Ms. Owner, is to teach and reward the pup for coming reliably, willingly and happily when called—and you have just three months to get it done. Unless adequately reinforced, your puppy's tendency to approach people will self-destruct by adolescence.

Call your dog ("Fido, come!"), open your arms (and maybe squat down) as a welcoming signal, waggle a treat or toy as a lure, and reward the puppydog when he comes running. Do not wait to praise the dog until he reaches you—he may come 95 percent of the way and then run off after some distraction. Instead, praise the dog's *first* step towards you and continue praising enthusiastically for *every* step he takes in your direction.

When the rapidly approaching puppy dog is three lengths away from impact, instruct him to sit ("Fido, sit!") and hold the lure in front of you in an outstretched hand to prevent him from hitting you midchest and knocking you flat on your back! As Fido decelerates to nose the lure, move the treat upwards and backwards just over his muzzle with an upwards motion of your extended arm (palm-upwards). As the dog looks up to follow the lure, he will sit down (if he jumps up, you are holding the lure too high). Praise the dog for sitting. Move backwards and call him again. Repeat this many times over, always praising when Fido comes and sits; on occasion, reward him.

For the first couple of trials, use a training treat both as a lure to entice the dog to come and sit and as a reward for doing so. Thereafter, try to use different items as lures and rewards. For example, lure the dog with a Kong or Frisbee but reward her with a food treat. Or lure the dog with a food treat but pat her and throw a tennis ball as a reward. After just a few repetitions, dispense with the lures and rewards; the dog will begin to respond willingly to your verbal requests and hand signals just for the prospect of praise from your heart and affection from your hands.

Instruct every family member, friend and visitor how to get the dog to come and sit. Invite people over for a series of pooch parties; do not keep the pup a secret— let other people enjoy this puppy, and let the pup enjoy other people. Puppydog parties are not only fun, they easily attract a lot of people to help *you* train *your* dog. Unless you teach your dog *how* to meet people, that is, to sit for greetings, no doubt the dog will resort to jumping up. Then you and the visitors will get annoyed, and the dog will be punished. This is not fair. *Send out those invitations for puppy parties and teach your dog to be mannerly and socially acceptable.*

Even though your dog quickly masters obedient recalls in the house, his reliability may falter when playing in the back yard or local park. Ironically, it is *the owner* who has unintentionally trained the dog *not* to respond in these instances. By allowing the dog to play and run around and otherwise have a good time, but then to call the dog to put him on leash to take him home, the dog quickly learns playing is fun but training is a drag. Thus, playing in the park becomes a severe distraction, which works against training. Bad news!

Instead, whether playing with the dog off leash or on leash, request him to come at frequent intervals— say, every minute or so. On most occasions, praise and pet the dog for a few seconds while he is sitting, then tell him to go play again. For especially fast recalls, offer a couple of training treats and take the time to praise and pet the dog enthusiastically before releasing him. The dog will learn that coming when called is not necessarily the end of the play session, and neither is it the end of the world; rather, it signals an enjoyable, quality time-out with the owner before resuming play once more. In fact, playing in the park now becomes a very effective life-reward, which works to facilitate training by reinforcing each obedient and timely recall. Good news!

Sit, Down, Stand and Rollover

Teaching the dog a variety of body positions is easy for owner and dog, impressive for spectators and extremely useful for all. Using lure-reward techniques, it is possible to train several positions at once to verbal commands or hand signals (which impress the socks off onlookers).

Sit and ***down***—the two control commands—prevent or resolve nearly a hundred behavior problems. For example, if the dog happily and obediently sits or lies down when requested, he cannot jump on visitors, dash out the front door, run around and chase its tail, pester other dogs, harass cats or annoy family, friends or strangers. Additionally, "sit" or "down" are better emergency commands for off-leash control.

It is easier to teach and maintain a reliable sit than maintain a reliable recall. *Sit* is the purest and simplest of commands—either the dog is sitting or he is not. If there is any change of circumstances or potential danger in the park, for example, simply instruct the dog to sit. If he sits, you have a number of options: allow the dog to resume playing when he is safe; walk up and put the dog on leash, or call the dog. The dog will be much more likely to come when called if he has already acknowledged his compliance by sitting. If the dog does not sit in the park—train him to!

Stand and ***rollover-stay*** are the two positions for examining the dog. Your veterinarian will love you to distraction if you take a little time to teach the dog to stand still and roll over and play possum. Also, your vet bills will be smaller. The rollover-stay is an especially useful command and is really just a variation of the down-stay: whereas the dog lies prone in the traditional down, she lies supine in the rollover-stay.

As with teaching come and sit, the training techniques to teach the dog to assume all other body positions on cue are user-friendly and dog-friendly. Simply give the appropriate request, lure the dog into the desired body position using a training treat or toy and then *praise* (and maybe reward) the dog as soon as he complies. Try not to touch the dog to get him to respond. If you teach the dog by guiding him into position, the dog will quickly learn that rump-pressure means sit, for example, but as yet you still have no control over your dog if he is just six feet away. It will still be necessary to teach the dog to sit on request. So do not make training a time-consuming two-step process; instead, teach the dog to sit to a verbal request or hand signal from the outset. Once the dog sits willingly when requested, by all means use your hands to pet the dog when he does so.

To teach *down* when the dog is already sitting, say "Fido, down!," hold the lure in one hand (palm down) and lower that hand to the floor between the dog's forepaws. As the dog lowers his head to follow the lure, slowly move the lure away from the dog just a fraction (in front of his paws). The dog will lie down as he stretches his nose forward to follow the lure. Praise the dog when he does so. If the dog stands up, you pulled the lure away too far and too quickly.

When teaching the dog to lie down from the standing position, say "down" and lower the lure to the floor as before. Once the dog has lowered his forequarters and assumed a play bow, gently and slowly move the lure *towards* the dog between his forelegs. Praise the dog as soon as his rear end plops down.

After just a couple of trials it will be possible to alternate sits and downs and have the dog energetically perform doggy push-ups. Praise the dog a lot, and after half a dozen or so push-ups reward the dog with a training treat or toy. You will notice the more energetically you move your arm—upwards (palm up) to get the dog to sit, and downwards (palm down) to get the dog to lie down—the more energetically the dog responds to your requests. Now try training the dog in silence and you will notice he has also learned to respond to hand signals. Yeah! Not too shabby for the first session.

To teach *stand* from the sitting position, say "Fido, stand," slowly move the lure half a dog-length away from the dog's nose, keeping it at nose level, and praise the dog as he stands to follow the lure. As soon

Using a food lure to teach sit, down and stand. 1) "Phoenix, Sit." 2) Hand palm upwards, move lure up and back over dog's muzzle. 3) "Good sit, Phoenix!" 4) "Phoenix, down." 5) Hand palm downwards, move lure down to lie between dog's forepaws. 6) "Phoenix, off. Good down, Phoenix!" 7) "Phoenix, sit!" 8) Palm upwards, move lure up and back, keeping it close to dog's muzzle. 9) "Good sit, Phoenix

"Phoenix, stand!" 11) Move lure away from dog at nose height, then lower it a tad. 12) "Phoenix,~~ Good stand, Phoenix!" 13) "Phoenix, down!" 14) Hand palm downwards, move lure down to lie ~~tw~~een dog's forepaws. 15) "Phoenix, off! Good down-stay, Phoenix!" 16) "Phoenix, stand!" 17) Move ~~lur~~e away from dog's muzzle up to nose height. 18) "Phoenix, off! Good stand-stay, Phoenix. Now we'll ~~ma~~ke the vet and groomer happy!"

as the dog stands, lower the lure to just beneath the dog's chin to entice him to look down; otherwise he will stand and then sit immediately. To prompt the dog to stand from the down position, move the lure half a dog-length upwards and away from the dog, holding the lure at standing nose height from the floor.

Teaching **rollover** is best started from the down position, with the dog lying on one side, or at least with both hind legs stretched out on the same side. Say "Fido, bang!" and move the lure backwards and alongside the dog's muzzle to its elbow (on the side of its outstretched hind legs). Once the dog looks to the side and backwards, very slowly move the lure upwards to the dog's shoulder and backbone. Tickling the dog in the goolies (groin area) often invokes a reflex-raising of the hind leg as an appeasement gesture, which facilitates the tendency to roll over. If you move the lure too quickly and the dog jumps into the standing position, have patience and start again. As soon as the dog rolls onto its back, keep the lure stationary and mesmerize the dog with a relaxing tummy rub.

To teach **rollover-stay** when the dog is standing or moving, say "Fido, bang!" and give the appropriate hand signal (with index finger pointed and thumb cocked in true Sam Spade fashion), then in one fluid movement lure him to first lie down and then rollover-stay as above.

Teaching the dog to **stay** in each of the above four positions becomes a piece of cake after first teaching the dog not to worry at the toy or treat training lure. This is best accomplished by hand feeding dinner kibble. Hold a piece of kibble firmly in your hand and softly instruct "Off!" Ignore any licking and slobbering *for however long the dog worries at the treat*, but say "Take it!" and offer the kibble *the instant* the dog breaks contact with his muzzle. Repeat this a few times, and then up the ante and insist the dog remove his muzzle for one whole second before offering the kibble. Then progressively refine your criteria and have the dog not touch your hand (or treat) for longer and longer periods on each trial, such as for two seconds, four seconds, then six, ten, fifteen, twenty, thirty seconds and so on. The dog soon learns: (1) worrying at the treat never gets results, whereas (2) noncontact is often rewarded after a variable time lapse.

Teaching *"Off!"* has many useful applications in its own right. Additionally, instructing the dog not to touch a training lure often produces spontaneous and magical stays. Request the dog to stand-stay, for example, and not to touch the lure. At first set your sights on a short two-second stay before rewarding the dog. (Remember, every long journey begins with a single step.) However, on subsequent trials, gradually and progressively increase the length of stay required to receive a reward. In no time at all your dog will stand calmly for a minute or so.

Relevancy Training

Once you have taught the dog what you expect her to do when requested to come, sit, lie down, stand, rollover and stay, the time is right to teach the dog *why* she should comply with your wishes. The secret is to have many (*many*) extremely short training interludes (two to five seconds each) at numerous (*numerous*) times during the course of the dog's day. Especially work with the dog immediately *before* the dog's good times and *during* the dog's good times. For example, ask your dog to sit and/or lie down each time before opening doors, serving meals, offering treats and tummy rubs; ask the dog to perform a few controlled doggy push-ups before letting her off-leash or throwing a tennis ball; and perhaps request the dog to sit-down-sit-stand-down-stand-rollover before inviting her to cuddle on the couch.

Similarly, request the dog to sit many times during play or on walks, and in no time at all the dog will be only too pleased to follow your instructions because he has learned that a compliant response heralds all sorts of goodies. Basically all you are trying to teach the dog is how to say please: "Please throw the tennis ball. Please may I snuggle on the couch."

Remember, whereas it is important to keep training interludes short, it is equally important to have many short sessions each and every day. The shortest (and most useful) session comprises asking the dog to sit and then go play during a play session. When trained this way, your dog will soon associate training with good times. In fact, the dog may be unable to distinguish between training and good times and, indeed, there should be no distinction. The warped concept that training involves forcing the dog to comply and/or dominating his will is totally at odds with the picture of a truly well-trained dog. In reality, enjoying a game of training with a dog is no different from enjoying a game of backgammon or tennis with a friend; and walking with a dog should be no different from strolling with buddies on the golf course.

Walk by Your Side

Many people attempt to teach a dog to heel by putting him on a leash and physically correcting the dog when he makes mistakes. There are a number of things seriously wrong with this approach, the first being that most people do not want precision heeling; rather, they simply want the dog to follow or walk by their side. Second, when physically restrained during "training," even though the dog may grudgingly mope by your side when "handcuffed" on leash, let's see what happens when he is off leash. History! The dog is in the next county because he never enjoyed walking with you on leash and you have no control over him off leash. So let's just teach the dog off leash from the outset to *want* to walk with us. Third, if the dog has not been trained to heel, it is a trifle hasty to think about punishing the poor dog for making mistakes and breaking heeling rules he didn't even know existed. This is simply not fair! Surely, if the dog had been adequately taught how to heel, he would seldom make mistakes and hence there would be no need to correct the dog. Remember, each mistake and each correction (punishment) advertise the trainer's inadequacy, not the dog's. The dog is not stubborn, he is not stupid and he is not bad. Even if he were, he would still require training, so let's train him properly.

Let's teach the dog to *enjoy* following us and to *want* to walk by our side offleash. Then it will be easier to teach high-precision off-leash heeling patterns if desired. After attaching the leash for safety on outdoor walks, but before going anywhere, it is necessary to teach the dog specifically not to pull. Now it will be much easier to teach on-leash walking and heeling because the dog already wants to walk with you, he is familiar with the desired walking and heeling positions and he knows not to pull.

FOLLOWING

Start by training your dog to follow you. Many puppies will follow if you simply walk away from them and maybe click your fingers or chuckle. Adult dogs may require additional enticement to stimulate them to follow, such as a training lure or, at the very least, a lively trainer. To teach the dog to follow: (1) keep walking and (2) walk away from the dog. If the dog attempts to lead or lag, change pace; slow down if the dog forges too far ahead, but speed up if he lags too far behind. Say "Steady!" or "Easy!" each time before you slow down and "Quickly!" or "Hustle!" each time before you speed up, and the dog will learn to change pace on cue. If the dog lags or leads too far, or if he wanders right or left, simply walk quickly in the opposite direction and maybe even run away from the dog and hide.

Practicing is a lot of fun; you can set up a course in your home, yard or park to do this. Indoors, entice the dog to follow upstairs, into a bedroom, into the bathroom, downstairs, around the living room couch, zig-zagging between dining room chairs and into the kitchen for dinner. Outdoors, get the dog to follow around park benches, trees, shrubs and along walkways and lines in the grass. (For safety outdoors, it is advisable to attach a long line on the dog, but never exert corrective tension on the line.)

Remember, following has a lot to do with attitude—*your* attitude! Most probably your dog will *not* want to follow Mr. Grumpy Troll with the personality of wilted lettuce. Lighten up—walk with a jaunty step, whistle a happy tune, sing, skip and tell jokes to your dog and he will be right there by your side.

BY YOUR SIDE

It is smart to train the dog to walk close on one side or the other—either side will do, your choice. When walking, jogging or cycling, it is generally bad news to have the dog suddenly cut in front of you. In fact, I train my dogs to walk "By my side" and "Other side"—both very useful instructions. It is possible to position the dog fairly accurately by looking to the appropriate side and clicking your fingers or slapping your thigh on that side. A precise positioning may be attained by holding a training lure, such as a chewtoy, tennis ball, or food treat. Stop and stand still several times throughout the walk, just as you would when window shopping or meeting a friend. Use the lure to make sure the dog slows down and stays close whenever you stop.

When teaching the dog to heel, we generally want her to sit in heel position when we stop. Teach heel

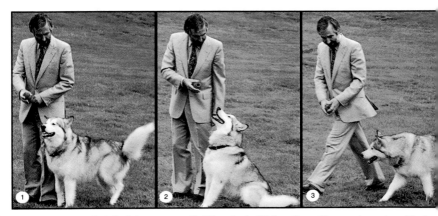

Using a toy to teach sit-heel-sit sequences: 1) "Phoenix, heel!" Standing still, move lure up and back over dog's muzzle.... 2) To position dog sitting in heel position on your left side. 3) "Phoenix, heel!" wagging lure in left hand. Change lure to right hand in preparation for sit signal.

position at the standstill and the dog will learn that the default heel position is sitting by your side (left or right—your choice, unless you wish to compete in obedience trials, in which case the dog must heel on the left).

Several times a day, stand up and call your dog to come and sit in heel position—"Fido, heel!" For example, instruct the dog to come to heel each time there are commercials on TV, or each time you turn a page of a novel, and the dog will get it in a single evening.

Practice straight-line heeling and turns separately. With the dog sitting at heel, teach him to turn in place. After each quarter-turn, half-turn or full turn in place, lure the dog to sit at heel. Now it's time for short straight-line heeling sequences, no more than a few steps at a time. Always think of heeling in terms of Sit-Heel-Sit sequences—start and end with the dog in position and do your best to keep him there when moving. Progressively increase the number of steps in each sequence. When the dog remains close for 20 yards of straight-line heeling, it is time to add a few turns and then sign up for a happy-heeling obedience class to get some advice from the experts.

4) Use hand signal only to lure dog to sit as you stop. Eventually, dog will sit automatically at heel whenever you stop. 5) "Good dog!"

No Pulling on Leash

You can start teaching your dog not to pull on leash anywhere—in front of the television or outdoors—but regardless of location, you must not take a single step with tension in the leash. For a reason known only to dogs, even just a couple of paces of pulling on leash is intrinsically motivating and diabolically rewarding. Instead, attach the leash to the dog's collar, grasp the other end firmly with both hands held close to your chest, and stand still—do not budge an inch. Have somebody watch you with a stopwatch to time your progress, or else you will never believe this will work and so you will not even try the exercise, and your shoulder and the dog's neck will be traumatized for years to come.

Stand still and wait for the dog to stop pulling, and to sit and/or lie down. All dogs stop pulling and sit eventually. Most take only a couple of minutes; the all-time record is 22 $\frac{1}{5}$ minutes. Time how long it takes. Gently praise the dog when he stops pulling, and as soon as he sits, enthusiastically praise the dog and take just one step forwards, then immediately stand still. This single step usually demonstrates the ballistic reinforcing nature of pulling on leash; most dogs explode to the end of the leash, so be prepared for the strain. Stand firm and wait for the dog to sit again. Repeat this half a dozen times and you will probably notice a progressive reduction in the force of the dog's one-step explosions and a radical reduction in the time it takes for the dog to sit each time.

As the dog learns "Sit we go" and "Pull we stop," she will begin to walk forward calmly with each single step and automatically sit when you stop. Now try two steps before you stop. Wooooooo! Scary! When the dog has mastered two steps at a time, try for three. After each success, progressively increase the number of steps in the sequence: try four steps and then six, eight, ten and twenty steps before stopping. Congratulations! You are now walking the dog on leash.

Whenever walking with the dog (off leash or on leash), make sure you stop periodically to practice a few position commands and stays before instructing the dog to "Walk on!" (Remember, you want the dog to be compliant everywhere, not just in the kitchen when his dinner is at hand.) For example, stopping every 25 yards to briefly train the dog amounts to over 200 training interludes within a single three-mile stroll. And each training session is in a different location. You will not believe the improvement within just the first mile of the first walk.

To put it another way, integrating training into a walk offers 200 separate opportunities to use the continuance of the walk as a reward to reinforce the dog's education. Moreover, some training interludes may comprise continuing education for the dog's walking skills: Alternate short periods of the dog walking calmly by your side with periods when the dog is allowed to sniff and investigate the environment. Now sniffing odors on the grass and meeting other dogs become rewards which reinforce the dog's calm and mannerly demeanor. Good Lord! Whatever next? Many enjoyable walks together of course. Happy trails!

THE IMPORTANCE OF TRICKS

Nothing will improve a dog's quality of life better than having a few tricks under its belt. Teaching any trick expands the dog's vocabulary, which facilitates communication and improves the owner's control. Also, specific tricks help prevent and resolve specific behavior problems. For example, by teaching the dog to fetch his toys, the dog learns carrying a toy makes the owner happy and, therefore, will be more likely to chew his toy than other inappropriate items.

More important, teaching tricks prompts owners to lighten up and train with a sunny disposition. Really, tricks should be no different from any other behaviors we put on cue. But they are. When teaching tricks, owners have a much sweeter attitude, which in turn motivates the dog and improves her willingness to comply. The dog feels tricks are a blast, but formal commands are a drag. In fact, tricks are so enjoyable, they may be used as rewards in training by asking the dog to come, sit and down-stay and then rollover for a tummy rub. Go on, try it: Crack a smile and even giggle when the dog promptly and willingly lies down and stays.

Most important, performing tricks prompts onlookers to smile and giggle. Many people are scared of dogs, especially large ones. And nothing can be more off-putting for a dog than to be constantly confronted by strangers who don't like him because of his size or the way he looks. Uneasy people put the dog on edge, causing him to back off and bark, only frightening people all the more. And so a vicious circle develops, with the people's fear fueling the dog's fear *and vice versa*. Instead, tie a pink ribbon to your dog's collar and practice all sorts of tricks on walks and in the park, and you will be pleasantly amazed how it changes people's attitudes toward your friendly dog. The dog's repertoire of tricks is limited only by the trainer's imagination. Below I have described three of my favorites:

SPEAK AND SHUSH

The training sequence involved in teaching a dog to bark on request is no different from that used when training any behavior on cue: request—lure—response—reward. As always, the secret of success lies in finding an effective lure. If the dog always barks at the doorbell, for example, say "Rover, speak!", have an accomplice ring the doorbell, then reward the dog for barking. After a few woofs, ask Rover to "Shush!", waggle a food treat under his nose (to entice him to sniff and thus to shush), praise him when quiet and eventually offer the treat as a reward. Alternate "Speak" and "Shush," progressively increasing the length of shush-time between each barking bout.

PLAYBOW

With the dog standing, say "Bow!" and lower the food lure (palm upwards) to rest between the dog's forepaws. Praise as the dog lowers her forequarters and sternum to the ground (as when teaching the down), but then lure the dog to stand and offer the treat. On successive trials, gradually increase the length of time the dog is required to remain in the playbow posture in order to gain a food reward. If the dog's rear end collapses into a down, say nothing and offer no reward; simply start over.

BE A BEAR

With the dog sitting backed into a corner to prevent him from toppling over backwards, say "Be a Bear!" With bent paw and palm down, raise a lure upwards and backwards along the top of the dog's muzzle. Praise the dog when he sits up on his haunches and offer the treat as a reward. To prevent the dog from standing on his hind legs, keep the lure closer to the dog's muzzle. On each trial, progressively increase the length of time the dog is required to sit up to receive a food reward. Since lure/reward training is so easy, teach the dog to stand and walk on his hind legs as well!

Teaching "Be a Bear"

chapter 9

Getting
Active
with your Dog

by Bardi McLennan

Once you and your dog have graduated from basic obedience training and are beginning to work together as a team, you can take part in the growing world of dog activities. There are so many fun things to do with your dog! Just remember, people and dogs don't always learn at the same pace, so don't be upset if you (or your dog) need more than two basic training courses before your team becomes operational. Even smart dogs don't go straight to college from kindergarten!

Just as there are events geared to certain types of dogs, so there are ones that are more appealing to certain types of people. In some activities, you give the commands and your dog does the work (upland game hunting is one example), while in others, such as agility, you'll both get a workout. You may want to aim for prestigious titles to add to your dog's name, or you may want nothing more than the sheer enjoyment of being around other people and their dogs. Passive or active, participation has its own rewards.

Consider your dog's physical capabilities when looking into any of the canine activities. It's easy to see that a Basset Hound is not built for the racetrack, nor would a Chihuahua be the breed of choice for pulling a sled. A loyal dog will attempt almost anything you ask him to do, so it is up to you to know your dog's limitations. A dog must be physically sound in order to compete at any level in athletic activities, and being mentally sound is a definite plus. Advanced age, however, may not be a deterrent. Many dogs still hunt and herd at ten or twelve years of age. It's entirely possible for dogs to be "fit at 50." Take your dog for a checkup, explain to your vet the type of activity you have in mind and be guided by his or her findings.

All dogs seem to love playing flyball.

You needn't be restricted to breed-specific sports if it's only fun you're after. Certain AKC activities are limited to designated breeds; however, as each new trial, test or sport has grown in popularity, so has the variety of breeds encouraged to participate at a fun level.

But don't shortchange your fun, or that of your dog, by thinking only of the basic function of her breed. Once a dog has learned how to learn, she can be taught to do just about anything as long as the size of the dog is right for the job and you both think it is fun and rewarding. In other words, you are a team.

To get involved in any of the activities detailed in this chapter, look for the names and addresses of the organizations that sponsor them in Chapter 13. You can also ask your breeder or a local dog trainer for contacts.

You can compete in obedience trials with a well trained dog.

Official American Kennel Club Activities

The following tests and trials are some of the events sanctioned by the AKC and sponsored by various dog clubs. Your dog's expertise will be rewarded with impressive titles. You can participate just for fun, or be competitive and go for those awards.

OBEDIENCE

Training classes begin with pups as young as three months of age in kindergarten puppy training, then advance to pre-novice (all exercises on lead) and go on to novice, which is where you'll start off-lead work. In obedience classes dogs learn to sit, stay, heel and come through a variety of exercises. Once you've got the basics down, you can enter obedience trials and work toward earning your dog's first degree, a C.D. (Companion Dog).

The next level is called "Open," in which jumps and retrieves perk up the dog's interest. Passing grades in competition at this level earn a C.D.X. (Companion Dog Excellent). Beyond that lies the goal of the most ambitious—Utility (U.D. and even U.D.X. or OTCh, an Obedience Champion).

AGILITY

All dogs can participate in the latest canine sport to have gained worldwide popularity for its fun and excitement, agility. It began in England as a canine version of horse show-jumping, but because dogs are more agile and able to perform on verbal commands, extra feats were added such as climbing, balancing and racing through tunnels or in and out of weave poles.

Many of the obstacles (regulation or homemade) can be set up in your own backyard. If the agility bug bites, you could end up in international competition!

For starters, your dog should be obedience trained, even though, in the beginning, the lessons may all be taught on lead. Once the dog understands the commands (and you do, too), it's as easy as guiding the dog over a prescribed course, one obstacle at a time. In competition, the race is against the clock, so wear your running shoes! The dog starts with 200 points and the judge deducts for infractions and misadventures along the way.

All dogs seem to love agility and respond to it as if they were being turned loose in a playground paradise. Your dog's enthusiasm will be contagious; agility turns into great fun for dog and owner.

FIELD TRIALS AND HUNTING TESTS

There are field trials and hunting tests for the sporting breeds—retrievers, spaniels and pointing breeds, and for some hounds—Bassets, Beagles and Dachshunds. Field trials are competitive events that test a dog's ability to perform the functions for which she was bred. Hunting tests, which are open to retrievers,

---

TITLES AWARDED BY THE AKC

Conformation: Ch. (Champion)

Obedience: CD (Companion Dog); CDX (Companion Dog Excellent); UD (Utility Dog); UDX (Utility Dog Excellent); OTCh. (Obedience Trial Champion)

Field: JH (Junior Hunter); SH (Senior Hunter); MH (Master Hunter); AFCh. (Amateur Field Champion); FCh. (Field Champion)

Lure Coursing: JC (Junior Courser); SC (Senior Courser)

Herding: HT (Herding Tested); PT (Pre-Trial Tested); HS (Herding Started); HI (Herding Intermediate); HX (Herding Excellent); HCh. (Herding Champion)

Tracking: TD (Tracking Dog); TDX (Tracking Dog Excellent)

Agility: NAD (Novice Agility); OAD (Open Agility); ADX (Agility Excellent); MAX (Master Agility)

Earthdog Tests: JE (Junior Earthdog); SE (Senior Earthdog); ME (Master Earthdog)

Canine Good Citizen: CGC

Combination: DC (Dual Champion—Ch. and Fch.); TC (Triple Champion—Ch., Fch., and OTCh.)

spaniels and pointing breeds only, are noncompetitive
and are a means of judging the dog's ability as well as
that of the handler.

Hunting is a very large and complex part of canine
sports, and if you own one of the breeds that hunts, the
events are a great treat for your dog and you. He gets
to do what he was bred for, and you get to work with
him and watch him do it. You'll be proud of and
amazed at what your dog can do.

Fortunately, the AKC publishes a series of booklets on
these events, which outline the rules and regulations
and include a glossary of the sometimes complicated
terms. The AKC also publishes newsletters for field tri-
alers and hunting test enthusiasts. The United Kennel
Club (UKC) also has informative materials for the
hunter and his dog.

*Retrievers and
other sporting
breeds get to do
what they're
bred to in hunt-
ing tests.*

HERDING TESTS AND TRIALS

Herding, like hunting, dates
back to the first known uses man
made of dogs. The interest in
herding today is widespread,
and if you own a herding breed,
you can join in the activity.
Herding dogs are tested for
their natural skills to keep a
flock of ducks, sheep or cattle
together. If your dog shows
potential, you can start at the
testing level, where your dog can
earn a title for showing an inherent herding ability.
With training you can advance to the trial level, where
your dog should be capable of controlling even difficult livestock in diverse situations.

LURE COURSING

The AKC Tests and Trials for Lure Coursing are open
to traditional sighthounds—Greyhounds, Whippets,

Borzoi, Salukis, Afghan Hounds, Ibizan Hounds and Scottish Deerhounds—as well as to Basenjis and Rhodesian Ridgebacks. Hounds are judged on overall ability, follow, speed, agility and endurance. This is possibly the most exciting of the trials for spectators, because the speed and agility of the dogs is awesome to watch as they chase the lure (or "course") in heats of two or three dogs at a time.

TRACKING

Tracking is another activity in which almost any dog can compete because every dog that sniffs the ground when taken outdoors is, in fact, tracking. The hard part comes when the rules as to what, when and where the dog tracks are determined by a person, not the dog! Tracking tests cover a large area of fields, woods and roads. The tracks are laid hours before the dogs go to work on them, and include "tricks" like cross-tracks and sharp turns. If you're interested in search-and-rescue work, this is the place to start.

This tracking dog is hot on the trail.

EARTHDOG TESTS FOR SMALL TERRIERS AND DACHSHUNDS

These tests are open to Australian, Bedlington, Border, Cairn, Dandie Dinmont, Smooth and Wire Fox, Lakeland, Norfolk, Norwich, Scottish, Sealyham, Skye, Welsh and West Highland White Terriers as well as Dachshunds. The dogs need no prior training for this terrier sport. There is a qualifying test on the day of the event, so dog and handler learn the rules on the spot. These tests, or "digs," sometimes end with informal races in the late afternoon.

Here are some of the extracurricular obedience and racing activities that are not regulated by the AKC or UKC, but are generally run by clubs or a group of dog fanciers and are often open to all.

Canine Freestyle This activity is something new on the scene and is variously likened to dancing, dressage or ice skating. It is meant to show the athleticism of the dog, but also requires showmanship on the part of the dog's handler. If you and your dog like to ham it up for friends, you might want to look into freestyle.

Lure coursing lets sighthounds do what they do best—run!

Scent Hurdle Racing Scent hurdle racing is purely a fun activity sponsored by obedience clubs with members forming competing teams. The height of the hurdles is based on the size of the shortest dog on the team. On a signal, one team dog is released on each of two side-by-side courses and must clear every hurdle before picking up its own dumbbell from a platform and returning over the jumps to the handler. As each dog returns, the next on that team is sent. Of course, that is what the dogs are supposed to do. When the dogs improvise (going under or around the hurdles, stealing another dog's dumbbell, and so forth), it no doubt frustrates the handlers, but just adds to the fun for everyone else.

Flyball This type of racing is similar, but after negotiating the four hurdles, the dog comes to a flyball box, steps on a lever that releases a tennis ball into the air, catches the ball and returns over the hurdles to the starting point. This game also becomes extremely fun for spectators because the dogs sometimes cheat by catching a ball released by the dog in the next lane. Three titles can be earned—Flyball Dog (F.D.), Flyball Dog Excellent (F.D.X.) and Flyball Dog Champion (Fb.D.Ch.)—all awarded by the North American Flyball Association, Inc.

Dogsledding The name conjures up the Rocky Mountains or the frigid North, but you can find dogsled clubs in such unlikely spots as Maryland, North Carolina and Virginia! Dogsledding is primarily for the Nordic breeds such as the Alaskan Malamutes, Siberian Huskies and Samoyeds, but other breeds can try. There are some practical backyard applications to this sport, too. With parental supervision, almost any strong dog could pull a child's sled.

Coming over the A-frame on an agility course.

These are just some of the many recreational ways you can get to know and understand your multifaceted dog better and have fun doing it.

chapter 10

Your Dog
and your
Family

by Bardi McLennan

Adding a dog automatically increases your family by one, no matter whether you live alone in an apartment or are part of a mother, father and six kids household. The single-person family is fair game for numerous and varied canine misconceptions as to who is dog and who pays the bills, whereas a dog in a houseful of children will consider himself to be just one of the gang, littermates all. One dog and one child may give a dog reason to believe they are both kids or both dogs.

Either interpretation requires parental supervision and sometimes speedy intervention.

As soon as one paw goes through the door into your home, Rufus (or Rufina) has to make many adjustments to become a part of your family. Your job is to make him fit in as painlessly as possible. An older dog may have some frame of reference from past experience, but to a 10-week-old puppy, everything is brand new: people, furniture, stairs, when and where people eat, sleep or watch TV, his own place and everyone else's space, smells, sounds, outdoors—everything!

Puppies, and newly acquired dogs of any age, do not need what we think of as "freedom." If you leave a new dog or puppy loose in the house, you will almost certainly return to chaotic destruction and the dog will forever after equate your homecoming with a time of punishment to be dreaded. It is unfair to give your dog what amounts to "freedom to get into trouble." Instead, confine him to a crate for brief periods of your absence (up to three or four hours) and, for the long haul, a workday for example, confine him to one untrashable area with his own toys, a bowl of water and a radio left on (low) in another room.

Lots of pets get along with each other just fine.

For the first few days, when not confined, put Rufus on a long leash tied to your wrist or waist. This umbilical cord method enables the dog to learn all about you from your body language and voice, and to learn by his own actions which things in the house are NO! and which ones are rewarded by "Good dog." House-training will be easier with the pup always by your side. Speaking of which, accidents do happen. That goal of "completely housetrained" takes up to a year, or the length of time it takes the pup to mature.

The All-Adult Family

Most dogs in an adults-only household today are likely to be latchkey pets, with no one home all day but the dog. When you return after a tough day on the job, the dog can and should be your relaxation therapy. But going home can instead be a daily frustration.

Separation anxiety is a very common problem for the dog in a working household. It may begin with whines and barks of loneliness, but it will soon escalate into a frenzied destruction derby. That is why it is so important to set aside the time to teach a dog to relax when left alone in his confined area and to understand that he can trust you to return.

Let the dog get used to your work schedule in easy stages. Confine him to one room and go in and out of that room over and over again. Be casual about it. No physical, voice or eye contact. When the pup no longer even notices your comings and goings, leave the house for varying lengths of time, returning to stay home for a few minutes and gradually increasing the time away. This training can take days, but the dog is learning that you haven't left him forever and that he can trust you.

Any time you leave the dog, but especially during this training period, be casual about your departure. No anxiety-building fond farewells. Just "Bye" and go! Remember the "Good dog" when you return to find everything more or less as you left it.

If things are a mess (or even a disaster) when you return, greet the dog, take him outside to eliminate, and then put him in his crate while you clean up. Rant and rave in the shower! *Do not* punish the dog. You were not there when it happened, and the rule is: Only punish as you catch the dog in the act of wrongdoing. Obviously, it makes sense to get your latchkey puppy when you'll have a week or two to spend on these training essentials.

Family weekend activities should include Rufus whenever possible. Depending on the pup's age, now is the time for a long walk in the park, playtime in the backyard, a hike in the woods. Socializing is as important as health care, good food and physical exercise, so visiting Aunt Emma or Uncle Harry and the next-door neighbor's dog or cat is essential to developing an out-going, friendly temperament in your pet.

If you are a single adult, socializing Rufus at home and away will prevent him from becoming overly protective of you (or just overly attached) and will also prevent such behavioral problems as dominance or fear of strangers.

Babies

Whether already here or on the way, babies figure larger than life in the eyes of a dog. If the dog is there first, let him in on all your baby preparations in the house. When baby arrives, let Rufus sniff any item of clothing that has been on the baby before Junior comes home. Then let Mom greet the dog first before introducing the new family member. Hold the baby down for the dog to see and sniff, but make sure some-one's holding the dog on lead in case of any sudden moves. Don't play keep-away or tease the dog with the baby, which only invites undesirable jump-ing up.

The dog and the baby are "family," and for starters can be treated almost as equals. Things rapidly change, however, especially when baby takes to creeping around on all fours on the dog's turf or, better yet, has yummy pudding all over her face and hands! That's when a lot of things in the dog's and baby's lives become more separate than equal.

Dogs are perfect confidants.

Toddlers make terrible dog owners, but if you can't avoid the combination, use patient discipline (that is, positive teaching rather than punishment), and use time-outs before you run out of patience.

A dog and a baby (or toddler, or an assertive young child) should never be left alone together. Take the dog with you or confine him. With a baby or youngsters in the house, you'll have plenty of use for that wonderful canine safety device called a crate!

Young Children

Any dog in a house with kids will behave pretty much as the kids do, good or bad. But even good dogs and good children can get into trouble when play becomes rowdy and active.

Legs bobbing up and down, shrill voices screeching, a ball hurtling overhead, all add up to exuberant frustration for a dog who's just trying to be part of the gang. In a pack of puppies, any legs or toys being chased would be caught by a set of teeth, and all the pups involved would understand that is how the game is played. Kids do not understand this, nor do parents tolerate it. Bring Rufus indoors before you have reason to regret it. This is time-out, not a punishment.

Teach children how to play nicely with a puppy.

You can explain the situation to the children and tell them they must play quieter games until the puppy learns not to grab them with his mouth. Unfortunately, you can't explain it that easily to the dog. With adult supervision, they will learn how to play together.

Young children love to tease. Sticking their faces or wiggling their hands or fingers in the dog's face is teasing. To another person it might be just annoying, but it is threatening to a dog. There's another difference: We can make the child stop by an explanation, but the only way a dog can stop it is with a warning growl and then with teeth. Teasing is the major cause of children being bitten by their pets. Treat it seriously.

Older Children

The best age for a child to get a first dog is between the ages of 8 and 12. That's when kids are able to accept some real responsibility for their pet. Even so, take the child's vow of "I will never *ever* forget to feed (brush, walk, etc.) the dog" for what it's worth: a child's good intention at that moment. Most kids today have extra lessons, soccer practice, Little League, ballet, and so forth piled on top of school schedules. There will be many times when Mom will have to come to the dog's rescue. "I walked the dog for you so you can set the table for me" is one way to get around a missed appointment without laying on blame or guilt.

Kids in this age group make excellent obedience trainers because they are into the teaching/learning process themselves and they lack the self-consciousness of adults. Attending a dog show is something the whole family can enjoy, and watching Junior Showmanship may catch the eye of the kids. Older children can begin to get involved in many of the recreational activities that were reviewed in the previous chapter. Some of the agility obstacles, for example, can be set up in the backyard as a family project (with an adult making sure all the equipment is safe and secure for the dog).

Older kids are also beginning to look to the future, and may envision themselves as veterinarians or trainers or show dog handlers or writers of the next Lassie best-seller. Dogs are perfect confidants for these dreams. They won't tell a soul.

Other Pets

Introduce all pets tactfully. In a dog/cat situation, hold the dog, not the cat. Let two dogs meet on neutral turf—a stroll in the park or a walk down the street—with both on loose leads to permit all the normal canine ways of saying hello, including routine sniffing, circling, more sniffing, and so on. Small creatures such as hamsters, chinchillas or mice must be kept safe from their natural predators (dogs and cats).

Festive Family Occasions

Parties are great for people, but not necessarily for puppies. Until all the guests have arrived, put the dog in his crate or in a room where he won't be disturbed. A socialized dog can join the fun later as long as he's not underfoot, annoying guests or into the hors d'oeuvres.

There are a few dangers to consider, too. Doors opening and closing can allow a puppy to slip out unnoticed in the confusion, and you'll be organizing a search party instead of playing host or hostess. Party food and buffet service are not for dogs. Let Rufus party in his crate with a nice big dog biscuit.

At Christmas time, not only are tree decorations dangerous and breakable (and perhaps family heirlooms), but extreme caution should be taken with the lights, cords and outlets for the tree lights and any other festive lighting. Occasionally a dog lifts a leg, ignoring the fact that the tree is indoors. To avoid this, use a canine repellent, made for gardens, on the tree. Or keep him out of the tree room unless supervised. And whatever you do, *don't* invite trouble by hanging his toys on the tree!

Car Travel

Before you plan a vacation by car or RV with Rufus, be sure he enjoys car travel. Nothing spoils a holiday quicker than a carsick dog! Work within the dog's comfort level. Get in the car with the dog in his crate or attached to a canine car safety belt and just sit there until he relaxes. That's all. Next time, get in the car, turn on the engine and go nowhere. Just sit. When that is okay, turn on the engine and go around the block. Now you can go for a ride and include a stop where you get out, leaving the dog for a minute or two.

On a warm day, always park in the shade and leave windows open several inches. And return quickly. It only takes 10 minutes for a car to become an overheated steel death trap.

Motel or Pet Motel?

Not all motels or hotels accept pets, but you have a much better choice today than even a few years ago. To find a dog-friendly lodging, look at *On the Road Again With Man's Best Friend,* a series of directories that detail bed and breakfasts, inns, family resorts and other hotels/motels. Some places require a refundable deposit to cover any damage incurred by the dog. More B&Bs accept pets now, but some restrict the size.

If taking Rufus with you is not feasible, check out boarding kennels in your area. Your veterinarian may offer this service, or recommend a kennel or two he or she is familiar with. Go see the facilities for yourself, ask about exercise, diet, housing, and so on. Or, if you'd rather have Rufus stay home, look into bonded petsitters, many of whom will also bring in the mail and water your plants.

chapter 11

Your Dog
and your
Community

by Bardi McLennan

Step outside your home with your dog and you are no longer just family, you are both part of your community. This is when the phrase "responsible pet ownership" takes on serious implications. For starters, it means you pick up after your dog—not just occasionally, but every time your dog eliminates away from home. That means you have joined the Plastic Baggy Brigade! You always have plastic sandwich bags in your pocket and several in the car. It means you teach your kids how to use them, too. If you think this is "yucky," just imagine what

the person (a non-doggy person) who inadvertently steps in the mess thinks!

Your responsibility extends to your neighbors: To their ears (no annoying barking); to their property (their garbage, their lawn, their flower beds, their cat—especially their cat); to their kids (on bikes, at play); to their kids' toys and sports equipment.

There are numerous dog-related laws, ranging from simple dog licensing and leash laws to those holding you liable for any physical injury or property damage done by your dog. These laws are in place to protect everyone in the community, including you and your dog. There are town ordinances and state laws which are by no means the same in all towns or all states. Ignorance of the law won't get you off the hook. The time to find out what the laws are where you live is now.

Be sure your dog's license is current. This is not just a good local ordinance, it can make the difference between finding your lost dog or not. Many states now require proof of rabies vaccination and that the dog has been spayed or neutered before issuing a license. At the same time, keep up the dog's annual immunizations.

Dressing your dog up makes him appealing to strangers.

Never let your dog run loose in the neighborhood. This will not only keep you on the right side of the leash law, it's the outdoor version of the rule about not giving your dog "freedom to get into trouble."

Good Canine Citizen

Sometimes it's hard for a dog's owner to assess whether or not the dog is sufficiently socialized to be accepted by the community at large. Does Rufus or Rufina display good, controlled behavior in public? The AKC's Canine Good Citizen program is available through many dog organizations. If your dog passes the test, the title "CGC" is earned.

The overall purpose is to turn your dog into a good neighbor and to teach you about your responsibility to your community as a dog owner. Here are the ten things your dog must do willingly:

1. Allow a stranger to handle him or her as a groomer or veterinarian would.
2. Accept a stranger stopping to chat with you.
3. Walk nicely on a loose lead.
4. Walk calmly through a crowd.
5. Sit and be petted by a stranger.
6. Sit and down on command.
7. Stay put when you move away.
8. Casually greet another dog.
9. React confidently to distractions.
10. Accept being tied up in a strange place and left alone for a few minutes.

Schools and Dogs

Schools are getting involved with pet ownership on an educational level. It has been proven that children who are kind to animals are humane in their attitude toward other people as adults.

A dog is a child's best friend, and so children are often primary pet owners, if not the primary caregivers. Unfortunately, they are also the ones most often bitten by dogs. This occurs due to a lack of understanding that pets, no matter how sweet, cuddly and loving, are still animals. Schools, along with parents, dog clubs, dog fanciers and the AKC, are working to change all that with video programs for children not only in grade school, but in the nursery school and pre-kindergarten age group. Teaching youngsters how to be responsible dog owners is important community work. When your dog has a CGC, volunteer to take part in an educational classroom event put on by your dog club.

Boy Scout Merit Badge

A Merit Badge for Dog Care can be earned by any Boy Scout ages 11 to 18. The requirements are not easy, but amount to a complete course in responsible dog care and general ownership. Here are just a few of the things a Scout must do to earn that badge:

Point out ten parts of the dog using the correct names.

Give a report (signed by parent or guardian) on your care of the dog (feeding, food used, housing, exercising, grooming and bathing), plus what has been done to keep the dog healthy.

Explain the right way to obedience train a dog, and demonstrate three comments.

Several of the requirements have to do with health care, including first aid, handling a hurt dog, and the dangers of home treatment for a serious ailment.

The final requirement is to know the local laws and ordinances involving dogs.

There are similar programs for Girl Scouts and 4-H members.

Local Clubs

Local dog clubs are no longer in existence just to put on a yearly dog show. Today, they are apt to be the hub of the community's involvement with pets. Dog clubs conduct educational forums with big-name speakers, stage demonstrations of canine talent in a busy mall and take dogs of various breeds to schools for class-room discussion.

The quickest way to feel accepted as a member in a club is to volunteer your services! Offer to help with something—anything—and watch your popularity (and your interest) grow.

Therapy Dogs

Once your dog has earned that essential CGC and reliably demonstrates a steady, calm temperament, you could look into what therapy dogs are doing in your area.

Therapy dogs go with their owners to visit patients at hospitals or nursing homes, generally remaining on leash but able to coax a pat from a stiffened hand, a smile from a blank face, a few words from sealed lips or a hug from someone in need of love.

Nursing homes cover a wide range of patient care. Some specialize in care of the elderly, some in the treatment of specific illnesses, some in physical therapy. Children's facilities also welcome visits from trained therapy dogs for boosting morale in their pediatric patients. Hospice care for the terminally ill and the at-home care of AIDS patients are other areas where this canine visiting is desperately needed. Therapy dog training comes first.

Your dog can make a difference in lots of lives.

There is a lot more involved than just taking your nice friendly pooch to someone's bedside. Doing therapy dog work involves your own emotional stability as well as that of your dog. But once you have met all the requirements for this work, making the rounds once a week or once a month with your therapy dog is possibly the most rewarding of all community activities.

Disaster Aid

This community service is definitely not for everyone, partly because it is time-consuming. The initial training is rigorous, and there can be no let-up in the continuing workouts, because members are on call 24 hours a day to go wherever they are needed at a moment's notice. But if you think you would like to be able to assist in a disaster, look into search-and-rescue work. The network of search-and-rescue volunteers is worldwide, and all members of the American Rescue Dog Association (ARDA) who are qualified to do this work are volunteers who train and maintain their own dogs.

Physical Aid

Most people are familiar with Seeing Eye dogs, which serve as blind people's eyes, but not with all the other work that dogs are trained to do to assist the disabled. Dogs are also specially trained to pull wheelchairs, carry school books, pick up dropped objects, open and close doors. Some also are ears for the deaf. All these assistance-trained dogs, by the way, are allowed anywhere "No Pet" signs exist (as are therapy dogs when properly identified). Getting started in any of this fascinating work requires a background in dog training and canine behavior, but there are also volunteer jobs ranging from answering the phone to cleaning out kennels to providing a foster home for a puppy. You have only to ask.

Making the rounds with your therapy dog can be very rewarding.

part four

Beyond
the
Basics

chapter 12

Recommended Reading

Books

ABOUT HEALTH CARE

Ackerman, Lowell. *Guide to Skin and Haircoat Problems in Dogs*. Loveland, Colo.: Alpine Publications, 1994.

Alderton, David. *The Dog Care Manual*. Hauppauge, N.Y.: Barron's Educational Series, Inc., 1986.

American Kennel Club. *American Kennel Club Dog Care and Training*. New York: Howell Book House, 1991.

Bamberger, Michelle, DVM. *Help! The Quick Guide to First Aid for Your Dog*. New York: Howell Book House, 1995.

Carlson, Delbert, DVM, and James Giffin, MD. *Dog Owner's Home Veterinary Handbook*. New York: Howell Book House, 1992.

DeBitetto, James, DVM, and Sarah Hodgson. *You & Your Puppy*. New York: Howell Book House, 1995.

Humphries, Jim, DVM. *Dr. Jim's Animal Clinic for Dogs*. New York: Howell Book House, 1994.

McGinnis, Terri. *The Well Dog Book*. New York: Random House, 1991.

Pitcairn, Richard and Susan. *Natural Health for Dogs*. Emmaus, Pa.: Rodale Press, 1982.

ABOUT DOG SHOWS

Hall, Lynn. *Dog Showing for Beginners*. New York: Howell Book House, 1994.

Nichols, Virginia Tuck. *How to Show Your Own Dog*. Neptune, N. J.: TFH, 1970.

Vanacore, Connie. *Dog Showing, An Owner's Guide*. New York: Howell Book House, 1990.

ABOUT TRAINING

Ammen, Amy. *Training in No Time*. New York: Howell Book House, 1995.

Baer, Ted. *Communicating With Your Dog*. Hauppauge, N.Y.: Barron's Educational Series, Inc., 1989.

Benjamin, Carol Lea. *Dog Problems*. New York: Howell Book House, 1989.

Benjamin, Carol Lea. *Dog Training for Kids*. New York: Howell Book House, 1988.

Benjamin, Carol Lea. *Mother Knows Best*. New York: Howell Book House, 1985.

Benjamin, Carol Lea. *Surviving Your Dog's Adolescence*. New York: Howell Book House, 1993.

Bohnenkamp, Gwen. *Manners for the Modern Dog*. San Francisco: Perfect Paws, 1990.

Dibra, Bashkim. *Dog Training by Bash*. New York: Dell, 1992.

Dunbar, Ian, PhD, MRCVS. *Dr. Dunbar's Good Little Dog Book*, James & Kenneth Publishers, 2140 Shattuck Ave. #2406, Berkeley, Calif. 94704. (510) 658–8588. Order from the publisher.

Dunbar, Ian, PhD, MRCVS. *How to Teach a New Dog Old Tricks*, James & Kenneth Publishers. Order from the publisher; address above.

Dunbar, Ian, PhD, MRCVS, and Gwen Bohnenkamp. Booklets on *Preventing Aggression; Housetraining; Chewing; Digging; Barking; Socialization; Fearfulness; and Fighting*, James & Kenneth Publishers. Order from the publisher; address above.

Evans, Job Michael. *People, Pooches and Problems*. New York: Howell Book House, 1991.

Kilcommons, Brian and Sarah Wilson. *Good Owners, Great Dogs*. New York: Warner Books, 1992.

McMains, Joel M. *Dog Logic—Companion Obedience*. New York: Howell Book House, 1992.

Rutherford, Clarice and David H. Neil, MRCVS. *How to Raise a Puppy You Can Live With*. Loveland, Colo.: Alpine Publications, 1982.

Volhard, Jack and Melissa Bartlett. *What All Good Dogs Should Know: The Sensible Way to Train*. New York: Howell Book House, 1991.

ABOUT BREEDING

Harris, Beth J. Finder. *Breeding a Litter, The Complete Book of Prenatal and Postnatal Care*. New York: Howell Book House, 1983.

Holst, Phyllis, DVM. *Canine Reproduction*. Loveland, Colo.: Alpine Publications, 1985.

Walkowicz, Chris and Bonnie Wilcox, DVM. *Successful Dog Breeding, The Complete Handbook of Canine Midwifery*. New York: Howell Book House, 1994.

About Activities

American Rescue Dog Association. *Search and Rescue Dogs*. New York: Howell Book House, 1991.

Barwig, Susan and Stewart Hilliard. *Schutzhund*. New York: Howell Book House, 1991.

Beaman, Arthur S. *Lure Coursing*. New York: Howell Book House, 1994.

Daniels, Julie. *Enjoying Dog Agility—From Backyard to Competition*. New York: Doral Publishing, 1990.

Davis, Kathy Diamond. *Therapy Dogs*. New York: Howell Book House, 1992.

Gallup, Davis Anne. *Running With Man's Best Friend*. Loveland, Colo.: Alpine Publications, 1986.

Habgood, Dawn and Robert. *On the Road Again With Man's Best Friend*. New England, Mid-Atlantic, West Coast and Southeast editions. Selective guides to area bed and breakfasts, inns, hotels and resorts that welcome guests and their dogs. New York: Howell Book House, 1995.

Holland, Vergil S. *Herding Dogs*. New York: Howell Book House, 1994.

LaBelle, Charlene G. *Backpacking With Your Dog*. Loveland, Colo.: Alpine Publications, 1993.

Simmons-Moake, Jane. *Agility Training, The Fun Sport for All Dogs*. New York: Howell Book House, 1991.

Spencer, James B. *Hup! Training Flushing Spaniels the American Way*. New York: Howell Book House, 1992.

Spencer, James B. *Point! Training the All-Seasons Birddog*. New York: Howell Book House, 1995.

Tarrant, Bill. *Training the Hunting Retriever*. New York: Howell Book House, 1991.

Volhard, Jack and Wendy. *The Canine Good Citizen*. New York: Howell Book House, 1994.

General Titles

Haggerty, Captain Arthur J. *How to Get Your Pet Into Show Business*. New York: Howell Book House, 1994.

McLennan, Bardi. *Dogs and Kids, Parenting Tips*. New York: Howell Book House, 1993.

Moran, Patti J. *Pet Sitting for Profit, A Complete Manual for Professional Success*. New York: Howell Book House, 1992.

Scalisi, Danny and Libby Moses. *When Rover Just Won't Do, Over 2,000 Suggestions for Naming Your Dog.* New York: Howell Book House, 1993.

Sife, Wallace, PhD. *The Loss of a Pet.* New York: Howell Book House, 1993.

Wrede, Barbara J. *Civilizing Your Puppy.* Hauppauge, N.Y.: Barron's Educational Series, 1992.

Magazines

The AKC GAZETTE, The Official Journal for the Sport of Purebred Dogs. American Kennel Club, 51 Madison Ave., New York, NY.

Bloodlines Journal. United Kennel Club, 100 E. Kilgore Rd., Kalamazoo, MI.

Dog Fancy. Fancy Publications, 3 Burroughs, Irvine, CA 92718

Dog World. Maclean Hunter Publishing Corp., 29 N. Wacker Dr., Chicago, IL 60606.

Videos

"SIRIUS Puppy Training," by Ian Dunbar, PhD, MRCVS. James & Kenneth Publishers, 2140 Shattuck Ave. #2406, Berkeley, CA 94704. Order from the publisher.

"Training the Companion Dog," from Dr. Dunbar's British TV Series, James & Kenneth Publishers. (See address above).

The American Kennel Club produces videos on every breed of dog, as well as on hunting tests, field trials and other areas of interest to purebred dog owners. For more information, write to AKC/Video Fulfillment, 5580 Centerview Dr., Suite 200, Raleigh, NC 27606.

chapter 13

Resources

Breed Clubs

Every breed recognized by the American Kennel Club has a national (parent) club. National clubs are a great source of information on your breed. You can get the name of the secretary of the club by contacting:

The American Kennel Club
51 Madison Avenue
New York, NY 10010
(212) 696-8200

There are also numerous all-breed, individual breed, obedience, hunting and other special-interest dog clubs across the country. The American Kennel Club can provide you with a geographical list of clubs to find ones in your area. Contact them at the above address.

Registry Organizations

Registry organizations register purebred dogs. The American Kennel Club is the oldest and largest in this country, and currently recognizes over 130 breeds. The United Kennel Club registers some breeds the AKC doesn't (including the American Pit Bull Terrier and the Miniature Fox Terrier) as well as many of the same breeds. The others included here are for your reference; the AKC can provide you with a list of foreign registries.

American Kennel Club
51 Madison Avenue
New York, NY 10010

United Kennel Club (UKC)
100 E. Kilgore Road
Kalamazoo, MI 49001-5598

American Dog Breeders Assn.
P.O. Box 1771
Salt Lake City, UT 84110
(Registers American Pit Bull Terriers)

Canadian Kennel Club
89 Skyway Avenue
Etobicoke, Ontario
Canada M9W 6R4

National Stock Dog Registry
P.O. Box 402
Butler, IN 46721
(Registers working stock dogs)

Orthopedic Foundation for Animals (OFA)
2300 E. Nifong Blvd.
Columbia, MO 65201-3856
(Hip registry)

Activity Clubs

Write to these organizations for information on the
activities they sponsor.

American Kennel Club
51 Madison Avenue
New York, NY 10010
(Conformation Shows, Obedience Trials, Field
Trials and Hunting Tests, Agility, Canine Good

Citizen, Lure Coursing, Herding, Tracking, Earthdog Tests, Coonhunting.)

United Kennel Club
100 E. Kilgore Road
Kalamazoo, MI 49001-5598
(Conformation Shows, Obedience Trials, Agility, Hunting for Various Breeds, Terrier Trials and more.)

North American Flyball Assn.
1342 Jeff St.
Ypsilanti, MI 48198

International Sled Dog Racing Assn.
P.O. Box 446
Norman, ID 83848-0446

North American Working Dog Assn., Inc.
Southeast Kreisgruppe
P.O. Box 833
Brunswick, GA 31521

Trainers

Association of Pet Dog Trainers
P.O. Box 3734
Salinas, CA 93912
(408) 663–9257

American Dog Trainers' Network
161 West 4th St.
New York, NY 10014
(212) 727–7257

National Association of Dog Obedience Instructors
2286 East Steel Rd.
St. Johns, MI 48879

Associations

American Dog Owners Assn.
1654 Columbia Tpk.
Castleton, NY 12033
(Combats anti-dog legislation)

Delta Society
P.O. Box 1080
Renton, WA 98057-1080
(Promotes the human/animal bond through
pet-assisted therapy and other programs)

Dog Writers Assn. of America (DWAA)
Sally Cooper, Secy.
222 Woodchuck Ln.
Harwinton, CT 06791

National Assn. for Search and Rescue (NASAR)
P.O. Box 3709
Fairfax, VA 22038

Therapy Dogs International
1536 Morris Place
Hillside, NJ 07205

6341026